Ten Steps TO A Federal Job

THIRD EDITION

Federal Jobs, Jobs, Jobs – Successful Federal
Job Search and Federal Resume Writing Strategies

Published by The Resume Place, Inc.
Baltimore, MD
Phone: (888) 480-8265
www.resume-place.com

Published by The Resume Place, Inc.
Baltimore, MD
Phone: (888) 480-8265
www.resume-place.com
Email: resume@resume-place.com

Copyright © 2011
Printed in the United States of America

ISBN: 978-0-9824190-6-9

AUTHOR'S NOTE:

Sample case studies are real, but fictionalized.
All federal applicants have given permission for their job application information to be used as samples for this publication. Privacy policy is strictly enforced.

PUBLICATION TEAM:

Cover Designer: Brian Moore
Interior Page Designer: Paulina Chen, LivingWaterDesigns, LLC
Developmental Editor/Technical Researcher: Paulina Chen
Proofreader: Pamela Sikora
Indexer: L. Pilar Wyman
Contributing Researchers/Writers: Emily K. Troutman and Sarah Blazucki

TABLE OF CONTENTS

ACKNOWLEDGMENTS

The one person who has contributed the most to the success of this book has been John Wallstone, the former Sous Chef, who is a real person (with a different name) and now works as a Program Analyst at FEMA today and has had several promotions since he began his career there in 2005. His federal job search story has inspired thousands to change careers because of his success.

Thank you to Sarah Blazucki, Certified Federal Resume Writer, who wrote the first federal resume for John. This outstanding federal resume resulted in a new career in government for the former chef. Thank you, Sarah, for your creativity, analysis, and writing skills.

Paulina Chen has been an invaluable Developmental Editor and Book Designer for all three editions. The first edition received recognition as Best Careers Book of the Year from Publisher's Marketing Association. These three editions and other books by The Resume Place, Inc., could never have been published without Paulina's technical, editorial, and design skills. Paulina also collaborated on and completed the Ten Steps eLearning curriculum, consisting of more than 100 short videos and audios. Thank you, Paulina, for your amazing patience, knowledge, and expertise.

Thank you to Bonny Day, Coordinator of the Certified Federal Job Search Trainer Program, which licenses and certifies career counselors and instructors worldwide to become Ten Step Trainers. The Ten Step Trainers are comprised of employment readiness counselors, transition counselors, workforce counselors, veteran's employment counselors and career counselors worldwide. The program and was established in 2002 and continues today through the Federal Career Training Institute, a division of The Resume Place, Inc. The colorful PowerPoint curriculum was designed by Paulina Chen and has been a popular, easy-to-teach program.

Thank you to Ed Palaszynski, Ph.D., for sponsoring the Ten Steps One Day Workshops since 2008 at Montgomery College Technology Center Information Technology Institute, Montgomery College, Gaithersburg, MD. Thousands of jobseekers attended classes in your state-of-the art computer classroom.

I want to thank Lex Levin for his co-teaching of the Ten Steps classes in Gaithersburg. He has inspired jobseekers to write KSAs, and then to add the KSAs into the resume. Also thanks to Greg Williams, Ph.D., from University of Maryland Baltimore County where he is Assistant Director, Instructional Design, for his early curriculum design for the Ten Steps eLearning course.

Thank you to my good friend Mike Causey for his support and writing of the Foreword on the next page. Federal job search *is* like fishing, and the more skilled you are, the bigger the fish you will catch (i.e., a great federal job). Listen to Mike at www.federalnewsradio.com. He is the voice of the federal employee.

Our sample federal resumes are now posted online and are available at www.resume-place.com. There you will find resumes of hundreds of real federal jobseekers who landed federal jobs. Thank you to Lisa Ford, Natalie Wood-Smith, Martin Frazier, Julie Kubiak, Cathy Sampson, Stephanie Gallahan, KeRita Anakoro, Jeff Clopein, Gary Bills, David Matthews, Philip Loftus, John Leszczynski, and Charlie McCoy for sharing your before and after resumes and federal job search stories. A very special thanks to Senior Federal Resume Writer and Analyst, Carla Waskiewicz, who who researched some of the best private industry to federal resume samples for your study and review.

It is certainly possible to catch fish without a hook, pole, or a worm. In fact, all you have to have are fish.

Our ancestors did it, that is, caught fish, by hand. And obviously it worked, because here we are. They did it for hundreds of thousands of years before somebody, possibly an ancestor of Kathryn Troutman, got wise. She invented string and connected the dots. A staffer came up with the all-important hook and the rest, as they say, is history.

But fishing by hand, while challenging, is not very rewarding and can be very dangerous. Based on their skeletons and fossil records, our prehistoric forefathers and foremothers were pretty skinny. Bottom line: this is why so few people today fish the old-fashioned way, even though it sometimes worked.

Which leads to the obvious question and even more obvious answer:

Question: Why do most fishermen use hook and line?

Answer: Because it works!

We have evolved from caves to cubicles. From loincloths to neckties. But despite these giant steps in human evolution, some people still hunt for a federal job the old-fashioned way. Like Ice Age hunters they read signs. Or they get an "inside" tip from a friend as to which agencies are biting. They read or hear that an agency mission is expanding. Or to minimize their possible commute, they go to the nearest federal agency's website and begin the hunt. They take the bait. And wait. And wait.

Increasingly smart people take another route to federal employment. They read *Ten Steps to a Federal Job*, by Kathryn Troutman. The first edition was an eye-opener (and proverbial hook, line, and sinker needed by job-hunters). This third edition is better yet. Think about the modern job strategist's version of Sun Tzu's *The Art of War*, a must-read if your war plan includes not losing.

Kathryn Troutman believes that getting a federal job today depends on careful planning. That getting onboard with Uncle Sam is no longer a matter of luck, being there at the right time, or knowing the right people. She believes it requires a campaign strategy. And this is a step-by-step guide that many, many people have found to be invaluable.

Now, if she would only come up with a diet-that-works for aging columnists, her place in history would be assured.

\- Mike Causey

FederalNewsRadio.com

PREFACE
by Kathryn K. Troutman

Ten Steps to a Federal Job™ is a step-by-step campaign approach to federal job search that helps jobseekers understand that government hiring is more complex than for a major corporation. The Ten Steps formula works. The federal job search isn't just "go to USAJOBS, find an announcement and submit your resume." You must take the critical steps before and after in order to succeed in your federal job search.

Ten Steps to a Federal Job™ was the first, accepted, structured federal job search curriculum ever created for instructors, career counselors, military transition offices, university career centers, federal human resources offices, or career training programs. The third edition still covers the original Ten Steps to a Federal Job™, which is now a popular course curriculum taught worldwide by hundreds of trainers we have certified, including those at more than 100 military bases and career centers on college campuses. The edition also still follows the Troutman Method for writing your federal resume, outlined on the next page. But this is where the similarities to the previous editions end.

The third edition of Ten Steps to a Federal Job is a more succinct "hiring reform" version that is about half the size of the second edition, down from 300 pages of text to about 150 pages. Federal Hiring Reform has created a shorter federal application with KSAs in the resume, and, in parallel, this book has also become more succinct. Due to the popularity of reading on the Kindle, Nook, iPad and even iPhone, we have reviewed every important page in the book and edited the text so that you can understand federal job search faster and easier on your electronic reader or computer.

This book also does NOT have a CD-ROM with case studies, as the second edition did. The one case study we kept was the famous Sous Chef case study, which is followed through the book to keep you focused on the transition from a simple private industry resume to the Outline Format federal resume that landed the Sous Chef a choice GS-11 Program Analyst position at FEMA, where he is now a GS-13.

The samples and case studies from the second edition are edited to include KSAs in the resume and are available online at www.resume-place.com as part of our incredible resource—the Online Federal Resume Database. While you are there, make sure to find the other federal job search resources that have made our website such a popular destination for jobseekers.

Finally, remember to send your federal job success story to me at kathryn@resume-place.com!

Sincerely,
Kathryn Troutman
Author, Trainer, and President
The Resume Place, Inc.

The Troutman Method

⊗ Accomplishments: Writing, remembering, and sharing accomplishments for your resume, KSAs, and preparation for Behavior-Based Interviews (Step 3 – Target Your Top Accomplishments)

⊗ Vacancy Announcements: Researching and interpreting vacancy announcements for keywords to be included in the federal resume and KSAs (Step 4 – Find the Perfect Job Announcement)

⊗ Keywords: Learning about the new Outline Format with keywords and headlines for resume builders (Step 5 – Identify Your Keywords)

⊗ Outline Format: Learning how to write your Outline Format USAJOBS resume (Step 6 – Master the Federal Resume)

⊗ KSAs with CCAR: Learning how to write KSAs that are impressive using the Context-Challenge-Action-Results formula, and how to cover the KSAs in the resume when that is required (Step 7 – Conquer the KSAs in the Resume and the Questionnaires)

I have developed a simple five point writing method, which I now call the "Troutman Method." I was thrilled to discover that the techniques I have honed over the last 15 years have come together into one awesome application approach to getting hired by the federal government.

This book is a clear introduction to the successful Troutman Method, which has been proven by thousands of individuals who have been referred for jobs, selected for interviews, and hired into federal careers. Countless times while I have taught these simple steps in the classroom or in consulting sessions, I have seen the light bulb go off when my client understood these techniques and could see why they would work. I hope that as you go through this book, your light bulb will also be lit, and you will be inspired to write the best possible federal resume for your job search.

INTRODUCTION
Make a Decision

Do you want to be a part of the change in government, the economy, jobs, and improved service to the American public? Do you want a stable, quality public service job where you can make a difference?

There are many good reasons why a person would want to work for the government. The federal government closely monitors employee satisfaction on factors such as pay, perks, location, infrastructure, training, supervision, fairness, and contribution to the agency's mission. The proof that most federal employees are satisfied with their jobs is the very high retention rate. Most feds stay feds. However, the process of getting hired is a key drawback. But remember that this book— *Ten Steps to a Federal Job*—and The Resume Place, Inc. can help make this process much easier for you.

This chapter will help you weigh these pros and cons to make the right decision about whether or not to pursue a government job.

Pros: Working for the Federal Government

✪ Job Security and Career Stability

The federal government is widely regarded as one of the most stable and reliable employers, especially in turbulent economic times. Federal employees have more job protection than their private sector counterparts, who may be fired at any time for any reason (or for no reason). Though occasionally "reductions in force," (RIFs) are instituted, outright termination is rare. Attrition and voluntary retirement incentives are usually the first line of action for any necessary "downsizing" before firings or layoffs. Once the employee's probationary period (usually a year) is over, most employees can be fired only for "cause," i.e., a performance or discipline-related issue. Review bodies such as the Merit Systems Protection Board, union membership, clear expectations, regular performance appraisals, and other mechanisms all help to ensure fairness in employment decisions.

✪ Competitive Pay

It is frequently thought that federal service pays less than the private sector. This assumption is not true in many of the cases we have seen when people made the jump from private industry to federal employment. Furthermore, if a person took a job with less annual salary (though not necessarily less in hourly pay when you consider the hours that some work in private industry), federal service is almost always still competitive with private industry jobs when you take into account the many benefits of federal employment. Some benefits can be assigned a dollar value, such as health benefits, family leave, vacation time, and holidays, while others are less tangible, but often equally important, such as job stability, lower levels of job stress, and flexible hours. Instead of competing against co-workers for raises, federal employees are generally awarded salary increases on a set schedule. An employee under the General Schedule usually receives annual increases for the first three years, followed by several biannual increases, and then increases every three years. Employees work their way up a scale of known salary hikes, and this system allows the employee to plan ahead. Federal employees also receive cost of living adjustments (COLAs) nearly every year, ranging from about 1.8% to 3.9%.

✪ Public Service / Mission-Oriented

According to the U.S. Merit Systems Protection Board, *Merit Principles Survey 2005,* "Results show that Federal employees are committed public servants."

- 94% believe that their agency's mission is important.

- 92% understand how their work contributes to the agency's overall mission.

- 86% find the work they do to be meaningful.

Recently, there has been more focus in the federal government on "linking" the work of each employee with specific aspects of the agency's mission. In this way, each employee understands what he or she contributes to the overall purpose of the agency, instead of feeling like just a cog in the wheel.

✪ Prestige, Pride, and History

Despite the notion that federal employees are just bureaucrats, most federal employees have a sense of pride in serving their government. To be a part, large or small, of the United States Government is an honor. To know that you are representing your country, can be very satisfying!

✪ Opportunity to Fight Terrorism

In the post-9/11 world, terrorism is no longer a far-away concept we see on the nightly news, unfolding in distant countries. Federal employment offers many opportunities to fight terrorism right here at home to keep America safe. These opportunities can be found not only in the armed forces or law enforcement agencies. For example, the U.S. Postal Service is on the front lines of ensuring that mail is not used to effectuate terrorist attacks.

✪ Transfers and Promotions

It is often said that the key to federal employment is to "get your foot in the door." In many cases, this is sage advice. For example, an attorney may give up a salary of $75,000 for a federal salary of $64,000, then get promoted in the next year or two, ending up with a salary of around $100,000. Thus, getting your foot in the door—getting a federal job in the first place—can position you for other opportunities such as promotions or transfers. Also, many agencies are generous in allowing voluntary or hardship transfers. The federal government has offices practically everywhere in America (and abroad), and this could be an important benefit if you should find yourself needing to relocate to take care of an elderly or sick relative, or if your spouse should get a great job offer in another town.

✪ Freedom from Discrimination

In the private sector, hiring and promotion decisions are supposed to be made free from unlawful discrimination on the basis of race, color, religion, sex, national origin, age, or disability. The federal sector takes this requirement very seriously, and aspires to be the example for the American workforce. If you suspect that the private sector has been turning you down for jobs on the basis of age or disability, or other unlawful basis, consider trying the federal sector.

✪ Disaster Assistance and Employee Assistance Programs (EAP)

The federal government demonstrates a real commitment to the safety, health, and well-being of its employees. During recent disasters such as Hurricane Katrina, the federal government allowed many of its employees to remain on payroll even when offices were closed. Agencies also invited their employees to take advantage of counseling and other services to enable employees to deal with the emotional, logistical, and financial fallout from such disasters. Agencies were flexible in allowing employees time off or modified schedules to deal with housing issues, contractors, insurance adjusters, and other disaster-related issues.

✪ Training Opportunities

Many agencies have a special budget for training, which not only better prepares employees for their current jobs, but positions them for advancement. Some training is online and can be conducted right from your desk. This training improves the employee's skills and their resume!

✪ Excellent Benefits

Federal benefits are among the best available anywhere, including vacation days, sick leave, leave donation programs, and retirement benefits. The health coverage is equal to or better than almost anything else around, and you can contribute your premiums in pretax dollars. Coverage for the employee and his or her family is very competitive! There are no medical examination requirements, age restrictions, exclusions for preexisting conditions, or waiting periods for benefits to begin.

The federal government also offers excellent life insurance and long-term disability insurance options.

The Flexible Spending Account (FSA) program reimburses employees for many non-covered medical expenditures and dependent-care costs. FSAs are effective financial management tools that can stretch the disposable incomes and ensure that funds are available, when needed, to pay for out-of-pocket medical costs or dependent-care expenses of a child or parent.

Check out this link for a great overview of federal job benefits: http://www.usajobs.gov/ei61.asp.

✪ Family and Medical Leave

The Family and Medical Leave Act (FMLA) requires covered employers to provide eligible employees up to 12 weeks of unpaid leave for the birth and care of the newborn child of the employee; for placement with the employee of a son or daughter through adoption or foster care; to care for an immediate family member (spouse, child, or parent) with a serious health condition; or to take medical leave when the employee is unable to work because of a serious health condition. Federal employees also enjoy "family-friendly leave policies," such as paid time off to serve as an organ donor or bone marrow donor, along with leave-sharing programs for sick employees who have used up their sick leave, and other benefits. Find out more at: http://www. opm.gov/oca/leave/index.asp.

✪ 401(k)-type Match Program

The Thrift Savings Program, similar to a 401(k), lets you save money in pre-tax dollars with substantial federal matching. Many experts consider it the best savings/investment program around. There are several options to choose from, including government funds that are considered very safe in economically turbulent times, and various funds geared to different retirement goals. Employees can also borrow against the TSP account. Find out more at www.tsp.gov.

✪ Flexible Work Schedules and Telecommuting

Most agencies allow flexible work hours that enable employees to take an extra day or two off every pay period. Flexible schedules can take the form of nine 9-hour days in a two-week period, with an extra day off in that period, or four 10-hour days with one day off every week.

Employees may also be able to opt for flexiplace. Employees on flexiplace, also called telecommuting, typically work at home, but can work at other agency-approved locations. For example, some agencies have telecommuting centers established in metropolitan areas for federal employees who would otherwise commute long distances between home and work. Telecommuting centers are furnished with the necessary office supplies and equipment.

✪ Transit Subsidy (in the Washington, D.C. Metropolitan Area)

This program can pay for most or all of the cost of public transit. In the D.C. area, subway transit is excellent. Save the wear and tear on your car, or go even greener and skip the car payment altogether!

✪ 10 Federal Holidays Each Year

How many people do you know in the private sector who are off for Columbus Day? Efficient and self-starting workers can get all their work done, earn an honest day's pay, and still have quite a lot of leisure time given the holidays, the flexible work hours, and the generous leave policies. Because the President ordains these holidays, you can enjoy these holidays off without guilt, and your boss will not frown—he or she will be off too! Stress-free time off from work is a major benefit of federal service.

The holidays are:
- New Year's Day
- Martin Luther King, Jr.'s Birthday
- Washington's Birthday
- Memorial Day
- Independence Day
- Labor Day
- Columbus Day
- Veterans Day
- Thanksgiving Day
- Christmas Day

✪ 13-26 Days of Leave Each Year (Depending on Years in Government)

The longer you serve, the more leave time you receive each year. By combining flexible work hours and leave, most federal employees work fewer hours per week than their private-sector counterparts. As long as your work gets done, many supervisors are very flexible about how you plan your time. Also, your boss will almost never make you give up your vacation plans for a last-minute emergency project, which is all too common in the private sector!

✪ Government Rates

Many public airline carriers and hotels provide government rates. In some cases, you are not required to be on official duty to take advantage of the government rate; simply show your government ID.

✪ Generosity

It is not widely known, but federal employees are among the most generous givers in America. The Combined Federal Campaign, a coordinated program of charitable giving, collects hundreds of thousands of dollars a year for important charities, such as helping the blind, conducting life-saving research, assisting veterans, among many others. In 2010, federal employees donated $281.5 million to thousands of organizations. Donations of any size can be made in lump sums or through relatively painless payroll deductions, and all donations are tax deductible. Sharing in this sense of community outreach and improvement of America through charitable giving is a meaningful benefit to federal employment.

✪ Other Benefits

Some agencies also offer tuition assistance, tuition reimbursement, extra pay for difficult-to-fill positions, relocation reimbursement, awards, bonuses, and other benefits. The website of each agency usually lists the benefits available. Specific benefits are also often listed in the vacancy announcement for each position.

Cons: The Federal Job Search

- The government as an employer is huge and intimidating; it is a challenge to understand how to "get in."

- The federal job application process is significantly different from the private sector; it will require substantial time and commitment to learn and execute the steps to landing a federal job.

- Novice federal jobseekers using materials they have prepared for the private sector usually do not get too far in their federal job search.

- Federal resumes are more detailed and complex to prepare. The average private industry resume is two pages. The average federal resume is three to four pages, and many applications require additional written responses to essay questions.

- A response to your federal application can take months. The government is working on an initiative to make a job offer within 45 days from the vacancy announcement closing date. This is a vast improvement from the past.

"Supervisors and upper level new employees believed that the hiring process was too complex and took too long. About a third of the new hires did not apply for other Federal jobs they were interested in because they would have had to write new essays or revise their existing essays describing their knowledge, skills and abilities; while about a fourth did not apply because they would have needed to rewrite or reformat their résumé." (Source: U.S. Merit Systems Protection Board, *In Search of Highly Skilled Workers; A Study on the Hiring of Upper Level Employees from Outside the Federal Government*, February 2008)

Good News: Job Growth in the Federal Government

The good news for those of you who still want to pursue a federal job—the jobs are out there. The following statistics demonstrate one of the reasons why the government will be hiring more from outside sources in the next 10 years.

- In September 2006, 40% of permanent full-time federal employees were 50 years of age or older.

- About 60% of the federal government's white-collar employees and 90% of the members of the Senior Executive Service will become eligible to retire within the next 10 years. (U.S. Merit Systems Protection Board, *Issues of Merit*, July 2007)

Besides hiring to backfill an aging workforce, the government must also hire to meet changing missions.

"Over the next two years, our largest federal agencies project that they will hire nearly 193,000 new workers for "mission-critical" jobs. While there are other federal jobs that will be filled during this time, including those in clerical and support positions, the jobs listed in this report constitute the bulk of our federal government's hiring needs. These jobs cover almost every occupational field, will be available across the country and all of them advance the interests of the American people. This report confirms that no matter what your area of expertise, or where you live, if you are looking for a job where you can develop your professional skills and make a difference in the lives of others, the federal government has a job for you." (Source: Partnership for Public Service, *Where the Jobs Are: Mission Critical Opportunities for America*, July 2007, http://ourpublicservice.org/OPS/publications/viewcontentdetails.php?id=118)

STEP ONE
Focus Your Federal Job Search

On any given day, there are more than 30,000 jobs posted on USAJOBS. In order to be successful, you need to focus your federal job search. You will need to narrow down which of these jobs you will invest your time applying for. To narrow your focus, you will need to take into account your interests, your qualifications, and the current hiring needs of the federal government.

Federal Job Statistics

Full-time federal civilian employees (excluding U.S. Postal Service and foreign nationals employed overseas)	1.85 million
Average age	46.9
Average length of service	16.3
Men	56%
Women	44%
Total minorities	32.1%
College degreed	43%
Average salary	$66,372
Average salary, DC metropolitan area	$86,444
White collar	89%
Largest Agency – Department of Defense	36%
Homeland Security	13%

Source: U.S. Office of Personnel Management, *Federal Civilian Workforce Statistics Fact Book*, 2007 Edition.

How Much Time Will a Typical Federal Application Take to Prepare?

Keep in mind that professional resume writers at Resume Place spend roughly eight to 10 hours preparing your first job application package without KSAs (Knowledge, Skills, and Abilities essays), and up to 15 hours preparing your first job application package with KSAs. Additional job applications require nearly two hours to research the vacancy announcements and edit your resume, and another three to five hours for KSAs and questionnaires. Of course, if you are new to the federal job search process, the application packages could take you longer to prepare on your own.

Searching for appropriate vacancy announcements could take an hour per day if you are serious about your federal job search campaign, but keep in mind that this investment could pay off tremendously for you.

Do I Have to be a U.S. Citizen to Apply For a Federal Job?

As a general rule, only U.S. citizens or nationals are eligible for competitive jobs in the civil service. This restriction was established by an executive order. In addition, Congress annually imposes a ban on using appropriated funds to hire noncitizens within the United States (certain groups of noncitizens are not included in this ban). Further, immigration law limits public and private sector hiring to only individuals who are 1) U.S. citizens or nationals; 2) aliens assigned by the U.S. Citizenship and Immigration Services (CIS) to a class of immigrants authorized to be employed (the largest group in this class is aliens lawfully admitted for permanent U.S. residence); or 3) an individual alien expressly authorized by the CIS to be employed.

Despite all of these limitations and restrictions, it is possible for noncitizens to obtain federal jobs in the U.S. For example, an agency may hire a qualified noncitizen in the excepted service or the Senior Executive Service if it is permitted to do so by the annual appropriations act and immigration law. And, if agencies cannot find qualified citizens to fill jobs in the competitive service, they may then hire noncitizens for those jobs. However, noncitizens may only be given an excepted appointment and will never acquire status. They may not be promoted or reassigned to another civil service job except in situations where qualified citizens are not available.

Do You Have the Skills the Government is Looking For?

You will greatly improve your chances of getting hired if you apply for jobs in the career field that the government is currently hiring. If you are applying for a job not listed on these tables, you could still find the job that you are looking for, but it may take you longer to get hired if there are only a few available openings.

New Hires by Occupation, FY 2007

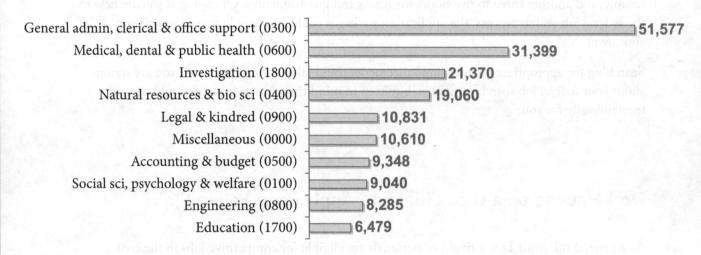

Source: U.S. Office of Personnel Management, *Table 18—Accessions by type, branch, and selected agency, all areas*, December 2006 and January 2007, http://www.opm.gov/feddata/html/2007/january/table18.asp.

Top 10 Occupations Posted on USAJOBS (as of June 27, 2011)

- ✪ Information Specialist
- ✪ Management and Program Analyst
- ✪ Administration & Program Staff
- ✪ Medical Officer
- ✪ Nurse
- ✪ Office Clerk / Assistant
- ✪ Contract Specialist
- ✪ Business and Industry Specialist
- ✪ Engineer, General
- ✪ Human Resources Specialist

To find the latest information on the top jobs being posted on USAJOBS, go to http://www.usajobs.gov/mostpopularjobs/index.asp.

Types of Federal Jobs

Job Classification

The different classes of jobs in the federal government each have different hiring practices. This information is important for you to strategize your application depending on the job type you are applying for. Ligaya Fernandez, retired Senior Personnel Policy Analyst, had this to say about the Occupational Families and Groups: "The government likes to create groups and categorize everything, so that we can analyze information, create reports and statistics." The government has neatly organized job families and job titles according to skill sets. This can help you find the job you are qualified for and stay organized in your federal job search.

Competitive Service Jobs

Competitive Service jobs are under U.S. Office of Personnel Management's (OPM) jurisdiction and follow laws to ensure that applicants and employees receive fair and equal treatment in the hiring process. Selecting officials have broad authority to review more than one applicant source before determining the best-qualified candidate based on job-related criteria. A basic principle of federal employment is that all candidates must meet the qualification requirements for the position for which they receive an appointment.

- ✪ Positions are open to the public. For positions lasting more than 120 days, vacancies must be announced and posted on USAJOBS, the federal government's central repository of job information.
- ✪ Applicants are rated against set criteria.
- ✪ Veterans' preference rules are applied.
- ✪ Candidates are ranked and referred in order, i.e., highest scoring candidates or candidates in the highest quality group are referred first for selection. However, compensable disabled veterans "float" to the top, except for scientific and professional upper-level positions.

In filling competitive service jobs, agencies can generally choose from among three groups of candidates:

Competitive list of eligibles, also known as the Cert List. This record lists the applicants (in rank order) who meet the qualification requirements for a specific vacancy announcement. Your primary objective is to get on the cert list, which means you will be referred to a supervisor for further consideration.

Eligibles with civil service status. This list consists of applicants who are already working for the federal government and are eligible for noncompetitive movement within the competitive service. They can receive an appointment by promotion, reassignment, transfer, or reinstatement.

Special noncompetitive eligibles. Examples of special noncompetitive appointing authorities include the Veterans' Readjustment Appointment (VRA), the special authority for 30% or more disabled veterans, and the Peace Corps.

Excepted Service Jobs

Excepted Service jobs are the jobs with agencies that set their own qualification requirements and are not subject to the appointment, pay, and classification rules in Title 5, United States Code. These excepted agencies are able to be more flexible with recruitment incentives, salaries, promotions, and other personnel matters. They are also subject to veterans' preference. Positions may be in the excepted service by law, executive order, or action of OPM. Some federal agencies, such as the Federal Bureau of Investigations (FBI) and the Central Intelligence Agency (CIA), have only excepted service positions. In other cases, certain organizations within an agency or even specific jobs may be excepted from civil service procedures.

Excepted service jobs are not required to be posted on USAJOBS. To learn about their job opportunities you must go to the specific agency websites. See a list of Excepted Service Positions and Excepted Service Agencies on the CD-ROM included with this book.

Direct Hire

Agencies use direct hiring when there is a shortage of qualified candidates, or when an agency has a critical hiring need, such as one caused by an emergency or unanticipated events, or changed mission requirements.

Direct hire provides a quick way to hire individuals in the competitive service. Although agencies are required to publicly post their vacancies on USAJOBS, they do not need to apply veterans' preference or rate and rank qualified candidates. Once a qualified candidate is found, agencies may offer the job on the spot and may appoint the candidate immediately.

OPM has allowed government-wide use of direct hire for the following occupations:

- ✪ Information technology management related to security
- ✪ X-ray technicians
- ✪ Medical officers, nurses, and pharmacists
- ✪ Positions involved in Iraqi reconstruction efforts requiring fluency in Arabic

Pathways Program and Other Student Hiring Programs

The government plans to implement the Pathways Program framework (www.opm.gov/hiringreform/pathways/) that President Obama signed into law on December 27, 2010. The Pathways framework is a group of two new programs (the Internships and Recent Graduate Programs) and an updated current program (the Presidential Management Fellowship) aimed at recruiting students and recent graduates into federal service. Although enacted last year, it is estimated that the Pathways framework will not take effect until late 2011 or early 2012. Our task in this step is to provide you with an overview of all the student opportunities and to prepare you for upcoming changes.

Other student federal hiring programs include: Student Temporary Employment Program (STEP); Student Career Experience Program (SCEP); Federal Work Study (FWS); Presidential Management Fellowship (PMF); Workforce Recruitment Program for College Students with Disabilities (WRP); and internships, scholarships, and grants. Your task is to identify which of these student programs is right for you. The better you know the information in this section, the more likely you will find a student position that could lead to a permanent federal job.

Decide on Agencies

To select an agency of interest to you, follow these steps:

- ✪ Conduct a mission statement match
- ✪ Determine location(s)
- ✪ Consider job availability

Mission Statement Match

Your choice to pursue a career in public service gives you the opportunity to choose an agency whose mission matches yours. Mission statements are often a practical guide and contain valuable information about each agency's goals, structure, and culture. Federal agencies are diverse and provide various services and missions for the American public. Reading the agency's mission statement is an important part of your federal job search. If you do not understand or know the agency's mission, you might not be successful with your application. To find mission statements, visit the homepage of any federal agency. You can find links to agencies at http://www.usa.gov/Agencies/Federal/All_Agencies/index.shtml.

Location, Location, Location

Contrary to popular belief, most federal jobs are NOT located only in Washington, DC. In fact, only 12% of the federal civilian workforce is located in the Washington, DC metropolitan area (U.S. Office of Personnel Management, *Federal Civilian Workforce Statistics Fact Book*, 2005 Edition). Federal government employment is available throughout the United States and overseas as well. You should ask yourself whether you are willing and able to relocate in order to expand your job search.

Job Availability

For job-seeking purposes, you can divide federal agencies into two categories—classic and hot. You can count on certain classic agencies to continually hire people with your skill set. For example, if you come from a business background, you might find jobs in agencies specializing in business services, such as the General Services Administration, the Small Business Administration, and the Department of Commerce. But remember, every federal agency has at least some employees who provide basic business services!

Some federal agencies simply hire more employees than others based on how much money is available and our nation's current employment focus. Such agencies are considered hot. As this book is written, the Department of Homeland Security (DHS) is definitely hot. As a result of recent national events, the department is experiencing significant hiring increases.

AGENCY LIST

A

Administration for Children and Families
Administration on Aging (AOA)
Administrative Office of the U.S. Courts
Advisory Council on Historic Preservation
Agency for Healthcare Research and Quality
Agency for International Development
Agency for Toxic Substances and Disease Registry
Agricultural Marketing Service
Agricultural Research Service
Air Force, Department of
AMTRAK (National Railroad Passenger
Corporation)
Animal and Plant Health Inspection Service
Appalachian Regional Commission
Architect of the Capitol
Armed Forces Retirement Home
Arms Control and International Security, Under
Secretary for
Army, Department of
Army Corps of Engineers (USACE)

B

Botanic Garden (USBG)
Broadcasting Board of Governors (BBG), (Voice of
America, Radio/TV Marti and more)
Bureau of Alcohol, Tobacco, Firearms, and
Explosives (ATF)
Bureau of Economic Analysis
Bureau of Engraving and Printing
Bureau of Indian Affairs
Bureau of Industry and Security
Bureau of International Labor Affairs
Bureau of Labor Statistics
Bureau of Land Management
Bureau of Public Debt
Bureau of Reclamation
Bureau of Transportation Statistics

C

Census Bureau
Center for Nutrition Policy and Promotion
Centers for Disease Control and Prevention (CDC)
Centers for Medicare & Medicaid Services
Central Intelligence Agency (CIA)
Citizenship and Immigration Services Bureau
(USCIS)
Civilian Radioactive Waste Management
Coast Guard (USCG)
Commission on Civil Rights
Community Oriented Policing Services
Community Planning and Development
Comptroller of the Currency, Office of the
Congressional Budget Office
Consumer Product Safety Commission (CPSC)

Cooperative State Research, Education and
Extension Service
Corporation for National and Community Service
Council of Economic Advisers
Council on Environmental Quality
Court of Appeals for the Armed Forces
Court of Appeals for the Federal Circuit
Court of Appeals for Veterans Claims
Court of Federal Claims
Court of International Trade
Customs and Border Protection

D

Defense Advanced Research Projects Agency
Defense Commissary Agency
Defense Contract Audit Agency
Defense Contract Management Agency
Defense Finance and Accounting Service
Defense Information Systems Agency
Defense Intelligence Agency (DIA)
Defense Legal Services Agency
Defense Logistics Agency
Defense Nuclear Facilities Safety Board
Defense Security Cooperation Agency
Defense Security Service
Defense Threat Reduction Agency
Department of Agriculture (USDA)
Department of Commerce (DOC)
Department of Defense (DOD)
Department of Education (ED)
Department of Energy (DOE)
Department of Health and Human Services (HHS)
Department of Homeland Security (DHS)
Department of Housing and Urban Development
(HUD)
Department of the Interior (DOI)
Department of Justice (DOJ)
Department of Labor (DOL)
Department of State (DOS)
Department of Transportation (DOT)
Department of the Treasury
Department of Veterans Affairs (VA)
Disability Employment Policy, Office of
Drug Enforcement Administration (DEA)

E

Economic and Statistics Administration
Economic, Business and Agricultural Affairs
Economic Development Administration
Economic Research Service
Elementary and Secondary Education, Office of
Employee Benefits Security Administration
Employment and Training Administration
Employment Standards Administration
Energy Efficiency and Renewable Energy
Energy Information Administration
Environmental Management
Environmental Protection Agency (EPA)

Equal Employment Opportunity Commission (EEOC)
Executive Office for Immigration Review

F
Fair Housing and Equal Opportunity, Office of
Faith-Based and Community Initiatives Office
Farm Service Agency (FSA)
Federal Aviation Administration
Federal Bureau of Investigation (FBI)
Federal Bureau of Prisons
Federal Communications Commission (FCC)
Federal Deposit Insurance Corporation (FDIC)
Federal Election Commission (FEC)
Federal Emergency Management Agency (FEMA)
Federal Financing Bank
Federal Highway Administration
Federal Housing Enterprise Oversight
Federal Housing Finance Board
Federal Judicial Center
Federal Labor Relations Authority
Federal Law Enforcement Training Center
Federal Mediation and Conciliation Service
Federal Motor Carrier Safety Administration
Federal Railroad Administration
Federal Reserve System
Federal Trade Commission (FTC)
Federal Transit Administration
Financial Management Service
Fish and Wildlife Service
Food and Drug Administration (FDA)
Food and Nutrition Service
Food Safety and Inspection Service
Foreign Agricultural Service
Forest Service
Fossil Energy

G
Government Accountability Office (GAO)
General Services Administration
Geological Survey (USGS)
Global Affairs
Government National Mortgage Association
Government Printing Office
Grain Inspection, Packers and Stockyards Administration

H
Health Resources and Services Administration
Holocaust Memorial Museum
House of Representatives
House Office of Inspector General
House Office of the Clerk
House Organizations, Commissions and Task Forces

I
Indian Health Service

Industrial College of the Armed Forces
Information Resource Management College
Institute of Museum and Library Services
Internal Revenue Service (IRS)
International Broadcasting Bureau (IBB)
International Trade Administration (ITA)

J
Joint Chiefs of Staff
Joint Forces Staff College
Judicial Circuit Courts of Appeal by Geographic Location and Circuit

L
Lead Hazard Control
Legal Services Corporation
Library of Congress

M
Marine Corps
Maritime Administration
Marketing and Regulatory Programs
Marshals Service
Merit Systems Protection Board
Mine Safety and Health Administration
Mineral Management Service
Minority Business Development Agency
Mint
Missile Defense Agency
Multifamily Housing Office

N
National Aeronautics and Space Administration (NASA)
National Agricultural Statistics Service
National Archives and Records Administration (NARA)
National Capital Planning Commission
National Cemetery Administration
National Commission on Terrorist Attacks Upon the United States (9-11 Commission)
National Communications System
National Council on Disability
National Credit Union Administration
National Defense University
National Drug Intelligence Center
National Endowment for the Arts
National Endowment for the Humanities
National Guard Bureau
National Highway Traffic Safety Administration
National Institute of Standards and Technology (NIST)
National Institutes of Health (NIH)
National Labor Relations Board
National Laboratories
National Marine Fisheries
National Mediation Board
National Nuclear Security Administration

Agency List Continued

National Oceanic and Atmospheric Administration (NOAA)
National Park Service
National Science Foundation
National Security Agency/Central Security Service
National Technical Information Service
National Telecommunications and Information Administration
National Transportation Safety Board (NTSB)
National War College
National Weather Service
Natural Resources Conservation Service
Navy, Department of the
Nuclear Energy, Science and Technology
Nuclear Regulatory Commission
Nuclear Waste Technical Review Board

O

Occupational Safety & Health Administration (OSHA)
Office of Government Ethics
Office of Management and Budget (OMB)
Office of National Drug Control Policy (ONDCP)
Office of Personnel Management
Office of Science and Technology Policy
Office of Special Counsel
Office of Thrift Supervision
Overseas Private Investment Corporation

P

Pardon Attorney Office
Parole Commission
Patent and Trademark Office
Peace Corps
Pension Benefit Guaranty Corporation
Policy Development and Research
Political Affairs
Postal Rate Commission
Postal Service (USPS)
Postsecondary Education, Office of
Power Marketing Administrations
Presidio Trust
Public Diplomacy and Public Affairs
Public and Indian Housing

R

Radio and TV Marti (Español)
Radio Free Asia (RFA)
Radio Free Europe/Radio Liberty (RFE/RL)
Railroad Retirement Board
Regulatory Information Service Center
Research and Special Programs Administration
Research, Education and Economics
Risk Management Agency

Rural Business-Cooperative Service
Rural Development
Rural Housing Service
Rural Utilities Service

S

Science Office
Secret Service
Securities and Exchange Commission (SEC)
Selective Service System
Senate
Small Business Administration (SBA)
Smithsonian Institution
Social Security Administration (SSA)
Social Security Advisory Board
Special Education and Rehabilitative Services
Stennis Center for Public Service
Student Financial Assistance Programs
Substance Abuse and Mental Health Services Administration
Supreme Court of the United States
Surface Mining, Reclamation and Enforcement
Surface Transportation Board

T

Tax Court
Technology Administration
Tennessee Valley Authority
Trade and Development Agency
Transportation Security Administration
Trustee Program

U

U.S. International Trade Commission
U.S. Mission to the United Nations
U.S. National Central Bureau – Interpol
U.S. Trade Representative
Unified Combatant Commands
Uniformed Services University of the Health Sciences

V

Veterans Benefits Administration
Veterans Employment and Training Service
Veterans Health Administration
Voice of America (VOA)

W

White House
White House Office of Administration
Women's Bureau

Review Job Titles and Occupational Series

The job titles are not the same in government as in private industry.

Before you can find vacancy announcements that are appropriate for your experience, education, and skills, you will need to know what the job titles entail. Some federal job titles mean something entirely different than in private industry. For instance, if you are a university researcher and writer, you could very well be qualified for a Management or Program Analyst position in government, yet how would you know this if you did not know the federal government's job title scheme?

You can find the *Handbook of Occupational Groups and Families*, May 2009 Edition at https://www.opm.gov/fedclass/gshbkocc.pdf to learn more about how the federal government organizes job categories.

Program Analysts and Management Analysts

These are popular job titles in federal agencies. Employees in these titles conduct analyses and advise management on the effectiveness of government programs and operations, or on the productivity and efficiency of agency management, or both. These jobs require knowledge of the substantive nature of agency programs and activities, knowledge of agency missions, policies, and objectives, management principles and processes, and analytical and evaluative techniques and methods. These jobs require skill in applying fact-finding and investigative techniques, oral and written communications, and development of presentations and reports. They do not require specialized subject-matter expertise in a specialized line of work.

Some Elusive Job Titles

Some job titles that seem familiar and carry a promise of exciting careers include Special Agent and Researcher, especially when the latter is used in medical or scientific settings such as the National Institutes of Health (NIH) or the Centers for Disease Control (CDC). But when we search for these titles, we do not find them. Why? Typically, these are working titles rather than official titles. As a result, they may not be used in vacancy announcements. So exercise your analytical and investigative skills and think investigator rather than special agent, especially criminal investigator (the government also has general investigators), for example.

On the following pages is a list of Occupational Groups and Series and Families that could provide you with some clues to your job title and series number for your job search. Two of the occupational groups are difficult to understand, but are important for private industry applicants. The 300-General Administrative and the 1100-Business and Industry Group series have a number of positions that equate well to private industry job experience.

OCCUPATIONAL GROUPS AND SERIES
FIND YOUR JOB TITLES

HANDBOOK OF OCCUPATIONAL GROUPS AND SERIES
U.S. Office of Personnel Management
Office of Classification; Washington, DC

GS-000 – MISCELLANEOUS OCCUPATIONS GROUP (NOT ELSEWHERE CLASSIFIED)

This group includes all classes of positions the duties of which are to administer, supervise, or perform work that cannot be included in other occupational groups either because the duties are unique, or because they are complex and come in part under various groups.

Series in this group are:
GS-006 - Correctional Institution Administration Series
GS-007 - Correctional Officer Series
GS-011 - Bond Sales Promotion Series
GS-018 - Safety and Occupational Health Management Series
GS-019 - Safety Technician Series
GS-020 - Community Planning Series
GS-021 - Community Planning Technician Series
GS-023 - Outdoor Recreation Planning Series
GS-025 - Park Ranger Series
GS-028 - Environmental Protection Specialist Series
GS-029 - Environmental Protection Assistant Series
GS-030 - Sports Specialist Series
GS-050 - Funeral Directing Series
GS-060 - Chaplain Series
GS-062 - Clothing Design Series
GS-072 - Fingerprint Identification Series
GS-080 - Security Administration Series
GS-081 - Fire Protection and Prevention Series
GS-082 - United States Marshal Series
GS-083 - Police Series
GS-084 - Nuclear Materials Courier Series
GS-085 - Security Guard Series
GS-086 - Security Clerical and Assistance Series
GS-090 - Guide Series
GS-095 - Foreign Law Specialist Series
GS-099 - General Student Trainee Series

GS-100 – SOCIAL SCIENCE, PSYCHOLOGY, AND WELFARE GROUP

This group includes all classes of positions the duties of which are to advise on, administer, supervise, or perform research or other professional and scientific work, subordinate technical work, or related clerical work in one or more of the social sciences; in psychology; in social work; in recreational activities; or in the administration of public welfare and insurance programs.

Series in this group are:
GS-101 - Social Science Series
GS-102 - Social Science Aid and Technician Series
GS-105 - Social Insurance Administration Series
GS-106 - Unemployment Insurance Series
GS-107 - Health Insurance Administration Series
GS-110 - Economist Series
GS-119 - Economics Assistant Series
GS-130 - Foreign Affairs Series
GS-131 - International Relations Series
GS-132 - Intelligence Series
GS-134 - Intelligence Aid and Clerk Series
GS-135 - Foreign Agricultural Affairs Series
GS-136 - International Cooperation Series
GS-140 - Manpower Research and Analysis Series
GS-142 - Manpower Development Series
GS-150 - Geography Series
GS-160 - Civil Rights Analysis Series
GS-170 - History Series
GS-180 - Psychology Series
GS-181 - Psychology Aid and Technician Series
GS-184 - Sociology Series
GS-185 - Social Work Series
GS-186 - Social Services Aid and Assistant Series
GS-187 - Social Services Series
GS-188 - Recreation Specialist Series
GS-189 - Recreation Aid and Assistant Series
GS-190 - General Anthropology Series
GS-193 - Archeology Series
GS-199 - Social Science Student Trainee Series

GS-200 – HUMAN RESOURCES MANAGEMENT GROUP

This group includes all classes of positions the duties of which are to advise on, administer, supervise, or perform work involved in the various phases of human resources management.

Series in this group are:
GS-201 - Human Resources Management Series
GS-203 - Human Resources Assistance Series
GS-241 - Mediation Series
GS-243 - Apprenticeship and Training Series
GS-244 - Labor Management Relations Examining Series

GS-260 - Equal Employment Opportunity Series
GS-299 - Human Resources Management Student Trainee Series

GS-300 – GENERAL ADMINISTRATIVE, CLERICAL, AND OFFICE SERVICES GROUP

This group includes all classes of positions the duties of which are to administer, supervise, or perform work involved in management analysis; stenography, typing, correspondence, and secretarial work; mail and file work; the operation of office appliances; the operation of communications equipment, use of codes and ciphers, and procurement of the most effective and efficient communications services; the operation of microform equipment, peripheral equipment, mail processing equipment, duplicating equipment, and copier/duplicating equipment; and other work of a general clerical and administrative nature.

Series in this group are:
GS-301 - Miscellaneous Administration and Program Series
GS-302 - Messenger Series
GS-303 - Miscellaneous Clerk and Assistant Series
GS-304 - Information Receptionist Series
GS-305 - Mail and File Series
GS-309 - Correspondence Clerk Series
GS-312 - Clerk-Stenographer and Reporter Series
GS-313 - Work Unit Supervising Series
GS-318 - Secretary Series
GS-319 - Closed Microphone Reporting Series
GS-322 - Clerk-Typist Series
GS-326 - Office Automation Clerical and Assistance Series
GS-332 - Computer Operation Series
GS-335 - Computer Clerk and Assistant Series
GS-340 - Program Management Series
GS-341 - Administrative Officer Series
GS-342 - Support Services Administration Series
GS-343 - Management and Program Analysis Series
GS-344 - Management and Program Clerical and Assistance Series
GS-346 - Logistics Management Series
GS-350 - Equipment Operator Series
GS-356 - Data Transcriber Series
GS-357 - Coding Series
GS-360 - Equal Opportunity Compliance Series
GS-361 - Equal Opportunity Assistance Series
GS-382 - Telephone Operating Series
GS-390 - Telecommunications Processing Series
GS-391 - Telecommunications Series
GS-392 - General Telecommunications Series
GS-394 - Communications Clerical Series
GS-399 - Administration and Office Support Student Trainee Series

GS-400 – NATURAL RESOURCES MANAGEMENT AND BIOLOGICAL SCIENCES GROUP

This group includes all classes of positions the duties of which are to advise on, administer, supervise, or perform research or other professional and scientific work or subordinate technical work in any of the fields of science concerned with living organisms, their distribution, characteristics, life processes, and adaptations and relations to the environment; the soil, its properties and distribution, and the living organisms growing in or on the soil, and the management, conservation, or utilization thereof for particular purposes or uses.

Series in this group are:
GS-401 - General Natural Resources Management and Biological Sciences Series
GS-403 - Microbiology Series
GS-404 - Biological Science Technician Series
GS-405 - Pharmacology Series
GS-408 - Ecology Series
GS-410 - Zoology Series
GS-413 - Physiology Series
GS-414 - Entomology Series
GS-415 - Toxicology Series
GS-421 - Plant Protection Technician Series
GS-430 - Botany Series
GS-434 - Plant Pathology Series
GS-435 - Plant Physiology Series
GS-437 - Horticulture Series
GS-440 - Genetics Series
GS-454 - Rangeland Management Series
GS-455 - Range Technician Series
GS-457 - Soil Conservation Series
GS-458 - Soil Conservation Technician Series
GS-459 - Irrigation System Operation Series
GS-460 - Forestry Series
GS-462 - Forestry Technician Series
GS-470 - Soil Science Series
GS-471 - Agronomy Series
GS-480 - Fish and Wildlife Administration Series
GS-482 - Fish Biology Series
GS-485 - Wildlife Refuge Management Series
GS-486 - Wildlife Biology Series
GS-487 - Animal Science Series
GS-499 - Biological Science Student Trainee Series

GS-500 – ACCOUNTING AND BUDGET GROUP

This group includes all classes of positions the duties of which are to advise on, administer, supervise, or perform professional, technical, or related clerical work of an accounting, budget administration, related financial management or similar nature.

Series in this group are:

GS-501 - Financial Administration and Program Series
GS-503 - Financial Clerical and Technician Series
GS-505 - Financial Management Series
GS-510 - Accounting Series
GS-511 - Auditing Series
GS-512 - Internal Revenue Agent Series
GS-525 - Accounting Technician Series
GS-526 - Tax Specialist Series
GS-530 - Cash Processing Series
GS-540 - Voucher Examining Series
GS-544 - Civilian Pay Series
GS-545 - Military Pay Series
GS-560 - Budget Analysis Series
GS-561 - Budget Clerical and Assistance Series
GS-592 - Tax Examining Series
GS-593 - Insurance Accounts Series
GS-599 - Financial Management Student Trainee Series

GS-600 – MEDICAL, HOSPITAL, DENTAL, AND PUBLIC HEALTH GROUP

This group includes all classes of positions the duties of which are to advise on, administer, supervise or perform research or other professional and scientific work, subordinate technical work, or related clerical work in the several branches of medicine, surgery, and dentistry or in related patient care services such as dietetics, nursing, occupational therapy, physical therapy, pharmacy, and others.

Series in this group are:
GS-601 - General Health Science Series
GS-602 - Medical Officer Series
GS-603 - Physician's Assistant Series
GS-610 - Nurse Series
GS-620 - Practical Nurse Series
GS-621 - Nursing Assistant Series
GS-622 - Medical Supply Aide and Technician Series
GS-625 - Autopsy Assistant Series
GS-630 - Dietitian and Nutritionist Series
GS-631 - Occupational Therapist Series
GS-633 - Physical Therapist Series
GS-635 - Kinesiotherapy Series
GS-636 - Rehabilitation Therapy Assistant Series
GS-637 - Manual Arts Therapist Series
GS-638 - Recreation/Creative Arts Therapist Series
GS-639 - Educational Therapist Series
GS-640 - Health Aid and Technician Series
GS-642 - Nuclear Medicine Technician Series
GS-644 - Medical Technologist Series
GS-645 - Medical Technician Series
GS-646 - Pathology Technician Series
GS-647 - Diagnostic Radiologic Technologist Series
GS-648 - Therapeutic Radiologic Technologist Series

GS-649 - Medical Instrument Technician Series
GS-650 - Medical Technical Assistant Series
GS-651 - Respiratory Therapist Series
GS-660 - Pharmacist Series
GS-661 - Pharmacy Technician Series
GS-662 - Optometrist Series
GS-664 - Restoration Technician Series
GS-665 - Speech Pathology and Audiology Series
GS-667 - Orthotist and Prosthetist Series
GS-668 - Podiatrist Series
GS-669 - Medical Records Administration Series
GS-670 - Health System Administration Series
GS-671 - Health System Specialist Series
GS-672 - Prosthetic Representative Series
GS-673 - Hospital Housekeeping Management Series
GS-675 - Medical Records Technician Series
GS-679 - Medical Support Assistance Series
GS-680 - Dental Officer Series
GS-681 - Dental Assistant Series
GS-682 - Dental Hygiene Series
GS-683 - Dental Laboratory Aid and Technician Series
GS-685 - Public Health Program Specialist Series
GS-688 - Sanitarian Series
GS-690 - Industrial Hygiene Series
GS-696 - Consumer Safety Series
GS-698 - Environmental Health Technician Series
GS-699 - Medical and Health Student Trainee Series

GS-700 - VETERINARY MEDICAL SCIENCE GROUP

This group includes positions that advise on, administer, supervise, or perform professional or technical support work in the various branches of veterinary medical science.

Series in this group are:
GS-701 - Veterinary Medical Science Series
GS-704 - Animal Health Technician Series
GS-799 - Veterinary Student Trainee Series

GS-800 – ENGINEERING AND ARCHITECTURE GROUP

This group includes all classes of positions the duties of which are to advise on, administer, supervise, or perform professional, scientific, or technical work concerned with engineering or architectural projects, facilities, structures, systems, processes, equipment, devices, materials or methods. Positions in this group require knowledge of the science or art, or both, by which materials, natural resources, and power are made useful.

Series in this group are:
GS-801 - General Engineering Series

GS-802 - Engineering Technician Series
GS-803 - Safety Engineering Series
GS-804 - Fire Protection Engineering Series
GS-806 - Materials Engineering Series
GS-807 - Landscape Architecture Series
GS-808 - Architecture Series
GS-809 - Construction Control Technical Series
GS-810 - Civil Engineering Series
GS-817 - Survey Technical Series
GS-819 - Environmental Engineering Series
GS-828 - Construction Analyst Series
GS-830 - Mechanical Engineering Series
GS-840 - Nuclear Engineering Series
GS-850 - Electrical Engineering Series
GS-854 - Computer Engineering Series
GS-855 - Electronics Engineering Series
GS-856 - Electronics Technical Series
GS-858 - Biomedical Engineering Series
GS-861 - Aerospace Engineering Series
GS-871 - Naval Architecture Series
GS-873 - Marine Survey Technical Series
GS-880 - Mining Engineering Series
GS-881 - Petroleum Engineering Series
GS-890 - Agricultural Engineering Series
GS-892 - Ceramic Engineering Series
GS-893 - Chemical Engineering Series
GS-894 - Welding Engineering Series
GS-895 - Industrial Engineering Technical Series
GS-896 - Industrial Engineering Series
GS-899 - Engineering and Architecture Student Trainee Series

GS-900 – LEGAL AND KINDRED GROUP

This group includes all positions that advise on, administer, supervise, or perform work of a legal or kindred nature.

Series in this group are:
GS-901 - General Legal and Kindred Administration Series
GS-904 - Law Clerk Series
GS-905 - General Attorney Series
GS-920 - Estate Tax Examining Series
GS-930 - Hearings and Appeals Series
GS-945 - Clerk of Court Series
GS-950 - Paralegal Specialist Series
GS-958 - Employee Benefits Law Series
GS-962 - Contact Representative Series
GS-963 - Legal Instruments Examining Series
GS-965 - Land Law Examining Series
GS-967 - Passport and Visa Examining Series
GS-986 - Legal Assistance Series
GS-987 - Tax Law Specialist Series
GS-991 - Workers' Compensation Claims Examining Series
GS-993 - Railroad Retirement Claims Examining Series

GS-996 - Veterans Claims Examining Series
GS-998 - Claims Assistance and Examining Series
GS-999 - Legal Occupations Student Trainee Series

GS-1000 – INFORMATION AND ARTS GROUP

This group includes positions that involve professional, artistic, technical, or clerical work in (1) the communication of information and ideas through verbal, visual, or pictorial means; (2) the collection, custody, presentation, display, and interpretation of art works, cultural objects, and other artifacts; or (3) a branch of fine or applied arts such as industrial design, interior design, or musical composition. Positions in this group require writing, editing, and language ability; artistic skill and ability; knowledge of foreign languages; the ability to evaluate and interpret informational and cultural materials; or the practical application of technical or esthetic principles combined with manual skill and dexterity; or related clerical skills.

Series in this group are:
GS-1001 - General Arts and Information Series
GS-1008 - Interior Design Series
GS-1010 - Exhibits Specialist Series
GS-1015 - Museum Curator Series
GS-1016 - Museum Specialist and Technician Series
GS-1020 - Illustrating Series
GS-1021 - Office Drafting Series
GS-1035 - Public Affairs Series
GS-1040 - Language Specialist Series
GS-1046 - Language Clerical Series
GS-1051 - Music Specialist Series
GS-1054 - Theater Specialist Series
GS-1056 - Art Specialist Series
GS-1060 - Photography Series
GS-1071 - Audiovisual Production Series
GS-1082 - Writing and Editing Series
GS-1083 - Technical Writing and Editing Series
GS-1084 - Visual Information Series
GS-1087 - Editorial Assistance Series
GS-1099 - Information and Arts Student Trainee Series

GS-1100 – BUSINESS AND INDUSTRY GROUP

This group includes all classes of positions the duties of which are to advise on, administer, supervise, or perform work pertaining to and requiring a knowledge of business and trade practices, characteristics and use of equipment, products, or property, or industrial production methods and processes, including the conduct of investigations and studies; the collection, analysis, and dissemination of information; the establishment and maintenance of contacts with industry and commerce; the provision of advisory services; the examination and appraisal of merchandise or property; and the administration of regulatory provisions and controls.

Series in this group are:
GS-1101 - General Business and Industry Series
GS-1102 - Contracting Series
GS-1103 - Industrial Property Management Series
GS-1104 - Property Disposal Series
GS-1105 - Purchasing Series
GS-1106 - Procurement Clerical and Technician Series
GS-1107 - Property Disposal Clerical and Technician Series
GS-1130 - Public Utilities Specialist Series
GS-1140 - Trade Specialist Series
GS-1144 - Commissary Management Series
GS-1145 - Agricultural Program Specialist Series
GS-1146 - Agricultural Marketing Series
GS-1147 - Agricultural Market Reporting Series
GS-1150 - Industrial Specialist Series
GS-1152 - Production Control Series
GS-1160 - Financial Analysis Series
GS-1163 - Insurance Examining Series
GS-1165 - Loan Specialist Series
GS-1169 - Internal Revenue Officer Series
GS-1170 - Realty Series
GS-1171 - Appraising Series
GS-1173 - Housing Management Series
GS-1176 - Building Management Series
GS-1199 - Business and Industry Student Trainee Series

GS-1200 – COPYRIGHT, PATENT, AND TRADEMARK GROUP

This group includes all classes of positions the duties of which are to advise on, administer, supervise, or perform professional scientific, technical, and legal work involved in the cataloging and registration of copyrights, in the classification and issuance of patents, in the registration of trademarks, in the prosecution of applications for patents before the Patent Office, and in the giving of advice to Government officials on patent matters.

Series in this group are:
GS-1202 - Patent Technician Series
GS-1210 - Copyright Series
GS-1220 - Patent Administration Series
GS-1221 - Patent Adviser Series
GS-1222 - Patent Attorney Series
GS-1223 - Patent Classifying Series
GS-1224 - Patent Examining Series
GS-1226 - Design Patent Examining Series
GS-1299 - Copyright and Patent Student Trainee Series

GS-1300 – PHYSICAL SCIENCES GROUP

This group includes all classes of positions the duties of which are to advise on, administer, supervise, or perform research or other professional and scientific work or subordinate technical work in any of the fields of science concerned with matter, energy, physical space, time, nature of physical measurement, and fundamental structural particles; and the nature of the physical environment.

Series in this group are:
GS-1301 - General Physical Science Series
GS-1306 - Health Physics Series
GS-1310 - Physics Series
GS-1311 - Physical Science Technician Series
GS-1313 - Geophysics Series
GS-1315 - Hydrology Series
GS-1316 - Hydrologic Technician Series
GS-1320 - Chemistry Series
GS-1321 - Metallurgy Series
GS-1330 - Astronomy and Space Science Series
GS-1340 - Meteorology Series
GS-1341 - Meteorological Technician Series
GS-1350 - Geology Series
GS-1360 - Oceanography Series
GS-1361 - Navigational Information Series
GS-1370 - Cartography Series
GS-1371 - Cartographic Technician Series
GS-1372 - Geodesy Series
GS-1373 - Land Surveying Series
GS-1374 - Geodetic Technician Series
GS-1380 - Forest Products Technology Series
GS-1382 - Food Technology Series
GS-1384 - Textile Technology Series
GS-1386 - Photographic Technology Series
GS-1397 - Document Analysis Series
GS-1399 - Physical Science Student Trainee Series

GS-1400 – LIBRARY AND ARCHIVES GROUP

This group includes all classes of positions the duties of which are to advise on, administer, supervise, or perform professional and scientific work or subordinate technical work in the various phases of library and archival science.

Series in this group are:
GS-1410 - Librarian Series
GS-1411 - Library Technician Series
GS-1412 - Technical Information Services Series
GS-1420 - Archivist Series
GS-1421 - Archives Technician Series

GS-1499 - Library and Archives Student Trainee Series

GS-1500 – MATHEMATICS AND STATISTICS GROUP

This group includes all classes of positions the duties of which are to advise on, administer, supervise, or perform professional and scientific work or related clerical work in basic mathematical principles, methods, procedures, or relationships, including the development and application of mathematical methods for the investigation and solution of problems; the development and application of statistical theory in the selection, collection, classification, adjustment, analysis, and interpretation of data; the development and application of mathematical, statistical, and financial principles to programs or problems involving life and property risks; and any other professional and scientific or related clerical work requiring primarily and mainly the understanding and use of mathematical theories, methods, and operations.

Series in this group are:
GS-1501 - General Mathematics and Statistics Series
GS-1510 - Actuarial Science Series
GS-1515 - Operations Research Series
GS-1520 - Mathematics Series
GS-1521 - Mathematics Technician Series
GS-1529 - Mathematical Statistics Series
GS-1530 - Statistics Series
GS-1531 - Statistical Assistant Series
GS-1540 - Cryptography Series
GS-1541 - Cryptanalysis Series
GS-1550 - Computer Science Series
GS-1599 - Mathematics and Statistics Student Trainee Series

GS-1600 – EQUIPMENT, FACILITIES, AND SERVICES GROUP

This group includes positions the duties of which are to advise on, manage, or provide instructions and information concerning the operation, maintenance, and use of equipment, shops, buildings, laundries, printing plants, power plants, cemeteries, or other Government facilities, or other work involving trades, crafts, or manual labor operations. Positions in this group require technical or managerial knowledge and ability, plus a practical knowledge of trades, crafts, or manual labor operations.

Series in this group are:
GS-1601 - Equipment, Facilities, and Services Series

GS-1603 - Equipment, Facilities, and Services Assistance Series
GS-1630 - Cemetery Administration Services Series
GS-1640 - Facility Operations Services Series
GS-1654 - Printing Services Series
GS-1658 - Laundry Operations Services Series
GS-1667 - Food Services Series
GS-1670 - Equipment Services Series
GS-1699 – Equipment, Facilities, and Services Student Trainee Series

GS-1700 – EDUCATION GROUP

This group includes positions that involve administering, managing, supervising, performing, or supporting education or training work when the paramount requirement of the position is knowledge of, or skill in, education, training, or instruction processes.

Series in this group are:
GS-1701 - General Education and Training Series
GS-1702 - Education and Training Technician Series
GS-1710 - Education and Vocational Training Series
GS-1712 - Training Instruction Series
GS-1715 - Vocational Rehabilitation Series
GS-1720 - Education Program Series
GS-1725 - Public Health Educator Series
GS-1730 - Education Research Series
GS-1740 - Education Services Series
GS-1750 - Instructional Systems Series
GS-1799 - Education Student Trainee Series

GS-1800 – INVESTIGATION GROUP

This group includes all classes of positions the duties of which are to advise on, administer, supervise, or perform investigation, inspection, or enforcement work primarily concerned with alleged or suspected offenses against the laws of the United States, or such work primarily concerned with determining compliance with laws and regulations.

Series in this group are:
GS-1801 - General Inspection, Investigation, and Compliance Series
GS-1802 - Compliance Inspection and Support Series
GS-1810 - General Investigating Series
GS-1811 - Criminal Investigating Series
GS-1812 - Game Law Enforcement Series
GS-1815 - Air Safety Investigating Series
GS-1816 - Immigration Inspection Series
GS-1822 - Mine Safety and Health Series
GS-1825 - Aviation Safety Series

GS-1831 - Securities Compliance Examining Series

GS-1850 - Agricultural Commodity Warehouse Examining Series

GS-1854 - Alcohol, Tobacco and Firearms Inspection Series

GS-1862 - Consumer Safety Inspection Series

GS-1863 - Food Inspection Series

GS-1864 - Public Health Quarantine Inspection Series

GS-1881 - Customs and Border Protection Interdiction Series

GS-1884 - Customs Patrol Officer Series

GS-1889 - Import Specialist Series

GS-1890 - Customs Inspection Series

GS-1894 - Customs Entry and Liquidating Series

GS-1895 - Customs and Border Protection Series

GS-1896 - Border Patrol Agent Series

GS-1897 - Customs Aid Series

GS-1899 - Investigation Student Trainee Series

GS-1900 – QUALITY ASSURANCE, INSPECTION, AND GRADING GROUP

This group includes all classes of positions the duties of which are to advise on, supervise, or perform administrative or technical work primarily concerned with the quality assurance or inspection of material, facilities, and processes; or with the grading of commodities under official standards.

Series in this group are:
GS-1910 - Quality Assurance Series
GS-1980 - Agricultural Commodity Grading Series
GS-1981 - Agricultural Commodity Aid Series
GS-1999 - Quality Inspection Student Trainee Series

GS-2000 – SUPPLY GROUP

This group includes positions that involve work concerned with furnishing all types of supplies, equipment, material, property (except real estate), and certain services to components of the Federal Government, industrial, or other concerns under contract to the Government, or receiving supplies from the Federal Government. Included are positions concerned with one or more aspects of supply activities from initial planning, including requirements analysis and determination, through acquisition, cataloging, storage, distribution, utilization to ultimate issue for consumption or disposal. The work requires a knowledge of one or more elements or parts of a supply system, and/or supply methods, policies, or procedures.

Series in this group are:
GS-2001 - General Supply Series
GS-2003 - Supply Program Management Series
GS-2005 - Supply Clerical and Technician Series
GS-2010 - Inventory Management Series
GS-2030 - Distribution Facilities and Storage Management Series
GS-2032 - Packaging Series
GS-2050 - Supply Cataloging Series
GS-2091 - Sales Store Clerical Series
GS-2099 - Supply Student Trainee Series

GS-2100 – TRANSPORTATION GROUP

This group includes all classes of positions the duties of which are to advise on, administer, supervise, or perform clerical, administrative, or technical work involved in the provision of transportation service to the Government, the regulation of transportation utilities by the Government, or the management of Government-funded transportation programs, including transportation research and development projects.

Series in this group are:
GS-2101 - Transportation Specialist Series
GS-2102 - Transportation Clerk and Assistant Series
GS-2110 - Transportation Industry Analysis Series
GS-2121 - Railroad Safety Series
GS-2123 - Motor Carrier Safety Series
GS-2125 - Highway Safety Series
GS-2130 - Traffic Management Series
GS-2131 - Freight Rate Series
GS-2135 - Transportation Loss and Damage Claims Examining Series
GS-2144 - Cargo Scheduling Series
GS-2150 - Transportation Operations Series
GS-2151 - Dispatching Series
GS-2152 - Air Traffic Control Series
GS-2154 - Air Traffic Assistance Series
GS-2161 - Marine Cargo Series
GS-2181 - Aircraft Operation Series
GS-2183 - Air Navigation Series
GS-2185 - Aircrew Technician Series
GS-2199 - Transportation Student Trainee Series

GS-2200 – INFORMATION TECHNOLOGY GROUP

Series in this group are:
GS-2210 - Information Technology Management Series
GS-2299 - Information Technology Student Trainee Series

Federal Grade and Pay Structure

The federal civil service has different grading and pay structures for its professional and trade workforces. In this book, we will focus on the professional jobs that the government categorizes in a system called PATCO (Professional, Administrative, Technical, Clerical, and Other). See definitions on the next page.

In many agencies, the professional jobs are organized into one of 15 grades in a system called the General Schedule (GS). General Schedule grades represent levels of difficulty and responsibility that are in fact defined by law. They are identified by the letters GS, followed by numbers, such as GS-1 (the lowest grade) to GS-15 (the highest). A recent graduate with a bachelor's degree would usually qualify for a GS-5 or 7.

Each GS grade has an associated base pay range that includes a minimum and a maximum rate of pay. There are ten pay rates between the base minimum and maximum. Base pay ranges are approximate (usually lower than actual salary) because a locality pay may be added depending on the city of employment, i.e., New York includes a locality pay. Both the base pay and locality pay are subject to adjustments each year, generally upward.

The GS Pay System

The ten rates for each GS grade are called steps. Movement through steps of a grade recognizes increased skill and knowledge level in the job. This contrasts with movement between grades, which really is a promotion involving taking on new, greater duties and responsibilities and getting paid more for doing so. Movement among steps is faster at the lower end of the scale, when people are learning more about their jobs. See the General Schedule pay scale on page 33.

Certain administrative and managerial positions have minimum requirements for education and experience based on the GS grade. The criteria involve either the education or experience minimums in combination or equivalency:

- **GS-5**: a four-year course of study above high school leading to a bachelor's degree; three years of general experience, with one year equivalent to GS-4

- **GS-7**: one full academic year of graduate-level education or superior academic achievement (college graduates in the upper third of their graduating class, with a minimum 3.0 GPA, or a member of a national scholastic honor society); one year of specialized experience at least equivalent to GS-5

- **GS-9**: two full academic years of graduate-level education or a master's degree; one year of specialized experience at least equivalent to GS-7

- **GS-11**: three full academic years of graduate-level education or a Ph.D.; one year of specialized experience at least equivalent to GS-9

- **GS-12**: one year of specialized experience at least equivalent to next lower grade level; no education requirements, as experience is considered the primary factor

PATCO

Federal jobs are made up of the following basic categories, titles, and grades:

Professional – GS-5 through 15

The professional positions have a POSITIVE EDUCATIONAL REQUIREMENT, including such occupations as chemist, accountant, doctor, engineer, social worker, or psychologist. Where there is an educational requirement, the education must meet standards set by the profession involved.

Administrative – GS-5 through 15

These jobs usually have the title of ANALYST or SPECIALIST. You can qualify for these jobs solely on the basis of experience, but below GS-12 education can be substituted for the required experience. If you have no experience, then you will need a degree to qualify for entry-level (GS-5 through 7) administrative positions. Certain law enforcement investigative and inspection positions are in this category: Special Agent, Border Patrol, Customs Inspector, and Immigration Inspector.

Technical – GS-6 through 9

These jobs are the TECHNICIAN or ASSISTANT positions, such as Accounting Technician or Assistant. Although a two- or four-year degree may be required in some fields (especially medical technician occupations), the primary qualifications requirement is experience. The Federal Aviation Administration Electronics Technician can be classified as high as a GS-12. Bachelor's degree graduates can qualify for Technician or Assistant positions starting at GS-7 with superior academic achievement.

Clerical – GS-1 through 5

These are the CLERK positions. There is no college degree requirement. An Associate of Arts degree graduate or two-year certification program graduate will qualify for GS-3 or 4 positions.

Other

This category includes jobs that do not fit other categories. It includes many law enforcement occupations, including security guard, police, ranger, park ranger, and U.S. Marshal, but does not include criminal investigators (special agent). Research psychologists and social scientists are also among the occupations in this category. The grades for this Other category can range from GS-3 to GS-15.

U.S. Office of Personnel Management, Salary Table 2011

Effective January 2011
http://www.opm.gov/oca/11tables/pdf/gs.pdf

Grade	Step 1	Step 2	Step 3	Step 4	Step 5	Step 6	Step 7	Step 8	Step 9	Step 10
1	$17,803	18,398	18,990	19,579	20,171	20,519	21,104	21,694	21,717	22,269
2	20,017	20,493	21,155	21,717	21,961	22,607	23,253	23,899	24,545	25,191
3	21,840	22,568	23,296	24,024	24,752	25,480	26,208	26,936	27,664	28,392
4	24,518	25,335	26,152	26,969	27,786	28,603	29,420	30,237	31,054	31,871
5	27,431	28,345	29,259	30,173	31,087	32,001	32,915	33,829	34,743	35,657
6	30,577	31,596	32,615	33,634	34,653	35,672	36,691	37,710	38,729	39,748
7	33,979	35,112	36,245	37,378	38,511	39,644	40,777	41,910	43,043	44,176
8	37,631	38,885	40,139	41,393	42,647	43,901	45,155	46,409	47,663	48,917
9	41,563	42,948	44,333	45,718	47,103	48,488	49,873	51,258	52,643	54,028
10	45,771	47,297	48,823	50,349	51,875	53,401	54,927	56,453	57,979	59,505
11	50,287	51,963	53,639	55,315	56,991	58,667	60,343	62,019	63,695	65,371
12	60,274	62,283	64,292	66,301	68,310	70,319	72,328	74,337	76,346	78,355
13	71,674	74,063	76,452	78,841	81,230	83,619	86,008	88,397	90,786	93,175
14	84,697	87,520	90,343	93,166	95,989	98,812	101,635	104,458	107,281	110,104
15	99,628	102,949	106,270	109,591	112,912	116,233	119,554	122,875	126,196	129,517

Pay Banding Pay Schedules

Now that we have covered the basic General Schedule grade and pay system, we must tell you that not every agency follows this pay system anymore. Pay banding, which allows an organization to combine two or more grades into a wider band, is an increasingly popular alternative to the traditional GS system. The grade information for jobs in agencies using pay banding will have a different look, and that look may be specific to a particular agency. Do not be surprised to see something as odd as ZP-1 or NO-II in place of GS-5 or GS-7. Focus rather on the duties, the salary, your qualifications for the job, and whether you want to pursue it. Remember, the federal government is large, and needs a way to increase flexibility of pay based on performance. Pay bands are their answer.

Examples of Pay Band Salaries

Department of Commerce, National Institute of Standards and Technology Pay Bands

	GS 1	GS 2	GS 3	GS 4	GS 5	GS 6	GS 7	GS 8	GS 9	GS 10	GS 11	GS 12	GS 13	GS 14	GS 15
ZA Administrative				1					2			3		4	5
ZP Professional				1					2			3		4	5
ZS Support		1		2		3		4		5					
ZT Technical			1				2				3		4	5	

Navy Research Lab

	GS 1	GS 2	GS 3	GS 4	GS 5	GS 6	GS 7	GS 8	GS 9	GS 10	GS 11	GS 12	GS 13	GS 14	GS 15	GS 16+
NP Scientist & Engineer Professional		I					II				III			IV		V
NR Scientist & Engineer Technical		I				II			III		IV	V				
NO Administrative Specialist/Prof.		I					II				III		IV	V		
NC Administrative Support		I			II			III								

How Federal Job Applications Are Processed

The number of resumes referred to the selecting official can range from three to 30, depending on the system. Key steps in federal hiring that involve job applicants' interaction:

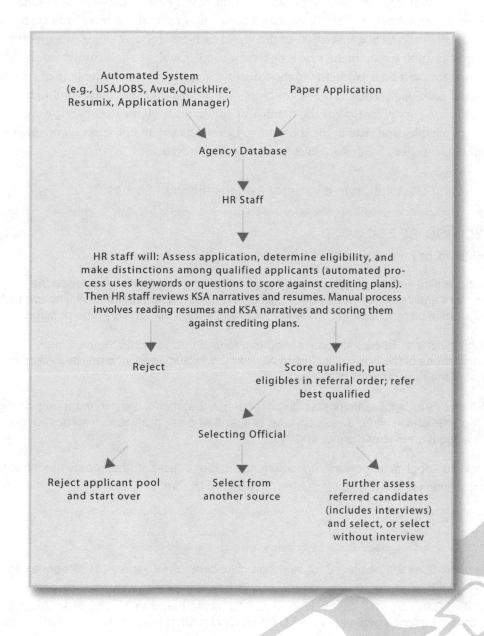

Category Rating–The New Federal Application Scoring System

Category rating is rapidly replacing the traditional numerical rating, ranking, and selection procedure, which used the commonly known "rule of three." The purpose of category rating is to increase the number of qualified applicants a hiring agency has to choose from while preserving veterans' preference. Applicants are assessed and sorted into at least two categories, and applicants with preference are moved to the top of each category. Veterans meeting the minimum qualification requirements and who have a compensable service-connected disability of at least 10 percent must be listed in the highest quality category (except in the case of scientific or professional positions at the GS-9 level or higher). Agencies may select any candidate in the highest quality category regardless of the number of applicants in that category. However, if there is a preference eligible candidate in the top category, the agency may not select a non-preference eligible candidate unless a request to do so is made and approved.

Category Rating Description in a Vacancy Announcement | Sample 1

HOW YOU WILL BE EVALUATED:

Applicants will be ranked based on four quality groups, as follows:

- Best qualified - applicants possessing experience that substantially exceeds the minimum qualifications of the position including all selective factors, and who are highly proficient in all requirements of the job and can perform effectively in the position;

- Highly qualified - applicants possessing experience that exceeds the minimum qualifications of the position including all selective factors, and who are proficient in most of the requirements of the job;

- Well qualified - applicants possessing experience that meets the minimum qualifications of the position including all selective factors, and who are proficient in some, but not all, of the requirements of the job; and

- Qualified - applicants possessing experience and/or education that meets the minimum qualifications of the position including all selective factors.

Sample 2

Eligible candidates will be placed for selection consideration into three (3) categories as described below:

1 - Qualified Category - Applicants who have a "Q" score between 70 and 84.99 meet the specialized experience outlined in the Minimum Qualification Requirements section of this announcement.

2 - Well Qualified Category - Applicants who have a "WQ" score between 85 and 94.99 exceed the Minimum Qualification Requirements based on review of resume and vacancy specific questions.

3 - Best Qualified Category - Applicants who have a "BQ" score between 95 and 100 Outstanding level based on review of resume and vacancy specific questions.

Do not overstate or understate your level of experience and capability. You should be aware that your ratings are subject to evaluation and verification.

How Can You Get Referred?

Under category rating, in order to be referred to a supervisor, you must meet the minimum qualifications and be ranked in the highest quality category. Here are eight ways that you can increase your chances of getting into the highest quality category.

1. **Keywords, keywords, keywords.** It always amazes me how basic this concept is, and yet, I still consult with many clients who are not putting the keywords into their applications. Look at the qualifications required in the vacancy announcement, and find and use the keywords in your resume where supportable. See Step 5 of this book for more examples and how-tos.

2. **Carefully read the Qualifications Required** section of the announcement to find out what you need to prove in your resume. Remember that you not only need to show that you are minimally-qualified, you also need to demonstrate that you are among the very best of the best, that you are an outstanding match for the job at hand.

3. **Show that you have at least one year of specialized experience** equivalent to at least the next lower grade level (at a level similar to the responsibilities of this job). Be clear and specific when describing your work experience. Federal HR will not make assumptions regarding your experience.

4. **Give proof** in your resume to support your questionnaire answers in order to receive credit.

5. **Get preference.** Veterans can add either 5 points or 10 points to their total application scores.

6. **KSAs are critical.** Prove that you have the KSAs for the position in your resume and questionnaire. See Step 7 on KSAs.

7. **Give yourself as much credit as possible** with the self-assessment questionnaires. In the example below, note that to rate yourself an E, you must have experience as an Expert, Supervisor, or Technical Advisor.

For each task in the following group, choose the statement from the list below that best describes your experience and/or training. Please select only one answer for each item.

Task: Communicate in areas of concern to service leadership and clinical staff as appropriate. Prepares reports for data collected, prepares correspondences related to licensed staff for credentialing, etc.

A- I have not had education, training or experience in performing this task.

B- I have had education or training in performing this task, but have not yet performed it on the job.

C- I have performed this task on the job. My work on this task was monitored closely by a supervisor or senior employee to ensure compliance with proper procedures.

D- I have performed this task as a regular part of a job. I have performed it independently and normally without review by a supervisor or senior employee.

E- I am considered an expert in performing this task. I have supervised performance of this task or am normally the person who is consulted by other workers to assist them in doing this task because of my expertise.

STEP TWO
Networking Success

Some people think that the only way you can apply for a federal job is through a posted vacancy announcement at www.usajobs.opm.gov or other federal job-posting sites.

You do not have to wait for your USAJOBS results. You can take some control with networking and the new email job search campaign approach that can help move your job search forward.

Networking Works

If you doubt that networking can help you land a job in the federal government, read this statistic:

"Some 45 percent of the new hires had first learned about their new Federal job from their friends and relatives (17 percent), their new Federal supervisors (15 percent), or their new Federal co-workers (13 percent). In comparison, only about a quarter (23 percent) of our respondents first learned about their Federal job through USAJOBS. Even fewer new hires first learned about their jobs through newspaper, journal, or magazine ads (2%) or from a Federal recruiter (1 percent). Friends and relatives were especially useful to new hires who previously were self-employed, unemployed, or working for a nonprofit or private company."

Source: U.S. Merit Systems Protection Board, *In Search of Highly Skilled Workers; A Study on the Hiring of Upper Level Employees from Outside the Federal Government,* February 2008.

Your contacts probably will not be able to get you a Federal job, but they can give you the information you need to know what is going on in an agency and when they might be hiring. Even if you use an electronic resume writing application to post your resume to a database, it helps to know people in the agency who know what jobs are coming up.

Identify Your Network – Friends and Family

Nearly everyone knows a federal employee or someone else who does. Do not be hesitant to introduce yourself to connections you are less familiar with. Simply introduce yourself and tell them that you have decided to begin your federal job search. Indicate that you know they work for the government, and that you would appreciate ten minutes of their time to talk about their job and their agency at their convenience. It is advisable to inquire about their job before asking how you could fit into their agency and whether their organization is hiring in the near future. Remember also to check with organizations you belong to. Locate your alumni membership list and look it over carefully. Who works for the government? Send them an email introduction as though they could be your next possible supervisor.

Government Networking—Getting Started with Self-Marketing

Be Bold

Start with people you know. Do not be embarrassed to cash in favors from family and friends. Send your introductory email to all of your friends and family members so they know what you have been doing for the last five years. Tell them what you are looking for, geographic locations you are open to, and the skills that you hope to use. Be enthusiastic, professional, and informative.

Do Your Research

Get to know people, missions, and agencies. Federal employees and managers are often more than happy to speak with potential candidates about their jobs, if you can find them online.

Government Executive Magazine – www.govexec.com – Read about federal employees and managers, including the Top Ten CEOs, CIOs, CFOs, and CHRMs. You can read about their background, agencies, missions, and objectives.

Partnership for Public Service – www.ourpublicservice.org – You can read about the Best Places to Work, Where the Jobs Are, Mission Critical Areas, and the winners of the Federal Employee of the Year award.

Agency Websites – My favorite pages include public affairs pages where you can read the latest press releases (what is totally new today/yesterday), mission statements, programs, customers, problems, offices, agencies, people who manage, and new initiatives. You can probably also find an organizational chart with names and titles in the website. This is a goldmine of information about people who run programs and who need talented employees like you to help them.

Do Not Expect a Miracle

Try to remember that a network is an opportunity to learn, but in the end the federal government cares about what you know, not who you know. In an online job search you have to handle rejection well. You have to be determined to make this work, follow-up, and look for another contact. Determination, perseverance, and initiative are critical core competencies for federal jobseekers.

Master the Email Informational Interview

In the old days, you might talk by phone or meet in person. The new informational interview is by email. The new online informational interview is simply an email to introduce oneself and ask one or two questions.

Suggested Questions to Ask in an Email Informational Interview
- What is your organization's mission?
- Is your organization growing or changing? If so, how?
- What qualifications are you seeking for any new hire?
- Will you be posting announcements in the near future?
- What are the top skills or attributes that you look for in a candidate in your organization?
- What other agencies do you work with?

Are You LinkedIn? Web Networking

Linkedin.com is an online network of more than 25 million professionals from around the world, representing 150 industries. When you join, you create a profile that summarizes your professional accomplishments. Your profile helps you find and be found by former colleagues, clients, and partners. You can add more connections by inviting trusted contacts to join LinkedIn and connect to you. This website is a great way to manage your network, keep your resume up-to-date, collect testimonials, broadcast your professional comings and goings, and stay in touch.

Federal Job Fairs

Government job fairs are increasing in number and are valuable opportunities to network. You may locate possible job leads, meet federal supervisors and human resources staff to get a sense of your audience, and see some of your competition. Do not go to the job fair as a spectator, but plan a strategy for a successful and informative job fair experience. Think of attending a job fair as walking into a mini-interview. You could be talking to the actual people who are making hiring decisions, so it is important for you to make a good first impression as an informed, credible, and motivated jobseeker.

Before you go to the job fair, do your research so that you know who to talk to and what to say.

- ✪ Go to the job fair website and find the list of attending federal agencies or government contractors.
- ✪ Select five or ten to focus on.
- ✪ Research these organizations online, finding out critical background information such as their mission and their main office locations.
- ✪ Decide which of these agencies you will approach at the job fair.
- ✪ Look up each agency in USAJOBS to see how many jobs it has listed currently.
- ✪ Get familiar with the job titles on the current announcements.

Job Fair Script

Review your resume and be prepared to make a short presentation to a job fair recruiter on the following key points:

- ✪ Your name
- ✪ Where you are from
- ✪ Where you last worked
- ✪ Your last job title
- ✪ Your top qualifications
- ✪ What you are seeking now
- ✪ Your availability
- ✪ Your message

The 1-2 Federal Networking/Application Campaign

The 1-2 Federal Networking/Application campaign is a new online job search system adapted for current times that is similar to the cold call job search approach from the 1960s through 1980s. In those days the cold call was very effective. A candidate would walk in the door, smile, say hi, leave a resume, develop a connection with a person in the office, and maybe even get an impromptu opportunity to meet the hiring supervisor.

Today, with stringent security measures at government agencies, the in-person cold call is not an option. Instead, there is another way to network: the government version of Web 2.0 networking. The new cold call campaign for government consists of an email introduction to your job application. By simply making email contact before you submit your application, you are taking a more proactive approach that is friendly, while adding a human element to your job search campaign. You will also connect with people in government.

Possible Results

With the 1-2 Federal Networking/Application campaign, the old adage definitely applies: it cannot hurt to try. On the other hand, going that extra mile could improve your chances of landing your target federal position.

When the supervisor receives your email, he or she might:

- ✪ Delete your email without responding.
- ✪ Look at the subject line and glance at your email, which should be impressive and short.
- ✪ Be looking for someone with your background and level of experience and write back to you regarding one of the following possible scenarios:
  - To start a dialogue about your background and the agency's mission.
  - To refer you to human resources who would advise you of forthcoming position openings.
  - To refer you to another program manager in the office, who might be interested in your background.
  - To advise you about upcoming job openings or announcements.

When an announcement that fits your background is posted in that agency and office, you could have already gained some tangible benefits by having sent an introductory email and standing out from the rest of the applicants. For example:

- ✪ When the supervisor receives the Certified List of Eligibles, he or she may already know your name, background, and education and might look for your name, knowing that you are interested in this type of position.
- ✪ When the supervisor reviews your resume, he or she will already know that you are interested, determined, personable, skilled, ready to work, and dedicated to the mission.

When to Use the 1-2 Approach

Open Inventory Announcements - These announcements have a long-term closing date and are basically resume collection vehicles. This database might be searched once a week just to see the submissions. The 1-2 Approach will let the supervisor know that you have put your resume into the Open Inventory Announcement, and that you will apply if there is a position that matches your qualifications. Examples of agencies that use the Open Inventory Announcements are the U.S. Navy, U.S. Marine Corps, and FBI.

Mission Specific - If you have a particular agency, office, and mission in mind for your federal career, then you should research this office and its manager. Learn the manager's name and write to them directly by email.

Geographic Preference – If you are relocating, or if you want to relocate to a certain city, state, or country, find agencies and offices in those locations. Locate the supervisors' names and departments, and write to them directly to introduce your background and interests.

Meet and Greet Anyone – If you want to introduce yourself to a certain supervisor (by email), just write about your interests and specialized background and see what happens.

Keep in mind that this approach might not work for Intelligence Agencies, because you may not be able to find names of managers or staff in these agencies. Networking for intelligence jobs will have to come through people you already know.

What to Include

Be sure to include the following in your email introduction: a short summary of your specialized knowledge, skills, education, and experience; the title of the position and the announcement number you are targeting so they can find you in the system; and an indication that you will also be submitting your resume into the "Open Inventory" Announcement process, if applicable.

Email Introduction Sample

Aaron D. West
Past Position: Instructional Systems Designer
Target Position: Instruction Systems Specialist, SV-1750; GS-11/12

SUBJECT: Request for Informational Interview for Aaron West on Instructional Systems Specialist Position

Dear Sir or Madam:

My name is Aaron D. West, and I am seeking a position as an Instructional Systems Specialist within the federal government. I would like to introduce my qualifications and specialized experience for consideration of this position in your agency. Having successfully performed as a Team Leader for multiple instructional design projects combined with my ability to assess, design, and produce effective training tools, I will prove to be an indispensible asset supporting the General Training and Career Programs within the Commodity Futures Trading Commission.

In addition to my federal resume, I have attached an addendum that describes a number of my recent projects in greater detail, including methodologies of the instructional design process.

- EXPERT in Instructional System Design. Fifteen years of experience in delivering instructional design solutions using a myriad of information technology tools and techniques.

- ANALYZE TRAINING NEEDS with Subject Matter Experts (SMEs) to ensure appropriate identification of learning requirements and delivery techniques.

- TEAM LEADER with ability to coordinate a variety of sources and integrate work products into a polished and comprehensive training course.

- USE ELEARNING AUTHORING TOOL to develop engaging and effective courses including Captive, Articulate, QuizMaker, Engage, and Lectora delivered via the Web and CD-ROM as well as instructor led programs.

I have formally applied to this position using the directions outlined in the USAJOBS announcement, but would like to communicate with you further to determine if this position would be a good fit. I would be more than happy to meet with you in person if it would be helpful. Thank you for your time, and I hope to hear from you soon.

Sincerely,
Aaron D. West

STEP THREE
Target Your Top Accomplishments

The hiring supervisor will be looking for accomplishments that demonstrate your skills and performance levels and give an indication of what your future performance will be in the job. Outstanding achievements can help your resume get noticed and land an interview.

The qualifications page of the job announcement will provide you a roadmap to understand what the hiring officials are looking for. Remember that to be considered for the position, you must have at least one year of specialized experience aligned with the skills and experience outlined in the qualifications page. Furthermore, in order to be referred, you need to demonstrate that you are outstanding in those same areas through—you guessed it—your accomplishments.

Troutman Method Lesson 1:
What Are Your Top Accomplishments?

After the federal job decision-making we have completed in the first two steps, we are now ready to get down to the task of creating an outstanding federal resume. It is time to think about YOU.

I find that many people have a difficult time getting started on writing their resumes, because they are either intimidated or bogged down with the daunting task of generating all the details that go into their resume, especially their federal resume.

My solution for easing into resume writing is to start first with the easiest—and most important—piece: your top accomplishments. Your top accomplishments will be the vital sound bites that you want to make sure are communicated to the people reviewing your job application.

Your top accomplishments will be used in the federal application process THREE TIMES:

- ✪ A short version of your accomplishments will be included in your federal resume (Step 6);
- ✪ A longer version will be drafted for the Knowledge, Skills, and Abilities narratives or essays that are required by the application questionnaires (Step 7); and
- ✪ You will review these accomplishments once again when you prepare for your Behavior-Based Interview (Step 10).

What Can Be Considered an Accomplishment?

Start with these basic questions when you are thinking about your accomplishments:

- ✪ What did you actually accomplish in your current job or previous job?
- ✪ What did you do that was outstanding – above average?
- ✪ Did you achieve something new or better?
- ✪ Did you save money for the organization?
- ✪ Did you come up with a new idea that saved time or improved customer service?

Two Types of Accomplishments

Let's start with the first type: *significant accomplishments*. Some examples are:

- ✪ Projects or teams you lead
- ✪ High profile situations
- ✪ Controversial or otherwise difficult situations / projects
- ✪ Unusually large projects
- ✪ Projects subject to very short deadlines
- ✪ Big problems you solved
- ✪ Important customer service solutions
- ✪ New training you implemented
- ✪ First time assignments or those requiring creativity to address
- ✪ Events or duties you performed that went far beyond your usual expected duties

The second general type of accomplishment is *tangible results*:

- ✪ Number of phone calls you answer in a day or week
- ✪ Number of emails you answer in a day or week
- ✪ Number of phone calls and emails you receive in a day or week
- ✪ Email management strategies created to improve the organization
- ✪ Number of times you update the budget in a week or month
- ✪ Number of invoices you process in a week or month
- ✪ Dollars you spend or handle in a week or month
- ✪ Number of appointments you make in a week or month for supervisors
- ✪ New Excel files you designed or managed each week or month

In some cases, your particular line of work may not have provided you the opportunity to engage in activities resulting in significant accomplishments. Instead, you might need to consider listing tangible results, otherwise known as bean counting. It may be difficult to quantify these numbers after the fact, but remember that demonstrating your accomplishments with numbers could greatly boost the impact of an accomplishment on your resume.

KSA Accomplishments Are Now Part of the Resume

Accomplishments in the resume are more important than ever. President Obama's federal hiring reform eliminated the separate narrative KSAs, but the KSA statements are still in the vacancy announcements.

Now the Human Resources Specialists state that the KSAs and accomplishments should be placed in the resume. Federal applications now are composed of two or three parts:

1. The federal resume - with KSA Accomplishments within the resume.

2. A questionnaire with self-assessment questions and sometimes essay narratives as a part of the application process. The questions could cover the KSAs that are required for the position.

3. Additional requested documents to provide proof of military service, federal status, or education-based qualifications if applicable.

Accomplishment Record / Top Ten List

Though it is not often used in federal hiring at this time, I find the concept of the accomplishment record to be very useful. When an accomplishment record is used, applicants will typically be asked to submit information on personal accomplishments to best illustrate their proficiency on critical job competencies (generally between four and eight). Specifically, applicants are often required to provide written descriptions of what was accomplished, including detailed information about the problem or situation, the specific actions taken, and the results or outcomes achieved by those actions. The name and contact information of an individual who can verify the statements is also usually required.

The accomplishment record is a way to collect information about applicants' training, education, experience, and past achievements related to critical job competencies. The idea is to view a record of past behavior as a predictor of future behavior.

For accomplishment records, accomplishments do not need to be only from work experience directly related to a vacancy announcement but can be accomplishments achieved in other jobs or through community service, school, volunteer work, military service, and even hobbies.

I've basically been teaching about the accomplishment record for many years now, except that I call it the Top Ten List of accomplishments. I recommend that you start to create your Top Ten List now and simply update it as you add new accomplishments. If you do so, you will have ample material to use for your KSAs, questionnaires, interviews, and yes, accomplishment records.

Develop a Project List with Results

As I explained on the previous page, a very useful regular work habit is to develop and track a list of accomplishments and projects. This information is invaluable for future job applications as well as during evaluation time.

Here is a suggested basic outline for your project or accomplishment list:
- Title of Project/Program
- Budget (if relevant)
- Role you played
- Mission, objective, purpose of project
- Customer/vendor
- Who you communicated or worked with to complete project
- Major challenge(s) or problem(s) during project
- Results (i.e., cost savings, increased efficiency, improved service to customers)

How Many Accomplishments Should I List?

Aim for a list of five to ten accomplishments.

What Kind of Format Should I Use?

There are two recommended formats for writing your top accomplishments:

Short Format

Write one or two sentences to summarize your best accomplishments for your resume. For more information about this format, see Step 7 on writing KSA accomplishments for the resume.

Longer Format: Top Ten List of Accomplishments

The Top Ten format is a full story about the accomplishment, so that you have a narrative to use in a KSA, essay, Executive Core Qualification (ECQ) narrative for Senior Executive Service positions, or job interview preparation. We have included examples of the longer format on the next two pages.

What Will I Do with this List?

Your top accomplishments will be the starting point for writing by helping you target the key messages in your resume and KSAs. You will improve on your accomplishments by adding keywords from the job announcements and the core competencies (see Step 5), and you will learn how to transform your list into your resume (see Step 6) and your KSAs (see Step 7).

Top Ten List of Accomplishments

These longer versions will be a first draft for a Knowledge, Skills, and Abilities narrative, a Questionnaire Essay, or an Executive Core Qualification Narrative. If you have many excellent accomplishments, you should write your Top Ten List with some details. In Step 7, we shorten these to an appropriate length for KSA accomplishments for your resume.

Examples

VICE-PRESIDENT OF MARKETING FOR A COMMUNICATIONS COMPANY. Participated in successful Initial Public Offering. Applied extensive financial expertise and practiced attention to detail so that IPO filings for Securities and Exchange Commission were up to date. Demonstrated skill in organizing materials quickly: Surgically rewrote marketing section changing bare minimum of words to bring document up to date without necessitating a rewrite of the entire document or pushing back schedule. RESULT: IPO was launched on-schedule, stock price rose 29% in following year.

MANAGER OF A SMALL VETERINARY CLINIC, ON A BOLD HUMAN RESOURCES DECISION. Hired person with no veterinary experience. It was her lifelong ambition to work with animals. Trained her in clerical duties, handling phone calls, scheduling appointments, and medical tasks such as dispensing pharmaceuticals, taking and analyzing x-rays, assisting in surgery, and sterilizing equipment. RESULT: This employee has now been with the clinic for two years and can ably perform essential medical procedures required of assistants.

CONTRACT SPECIALIST, SUCCESSFULLY MARKETED EDUCATIONAL MATERIALS. Negotiated, wrote, and managed contract with Centers for Disease Control (CDC) for AIDS/HIV awareness campaign. Identified CDC need to deliver message to five distinct communities. Wrote Scope of Work (SOW), calling for educational materials translated into five languages, illustrations to match ethnic appearances, and matching of language to Bush Administration Guidelines. RESULT: Materials well-received and regularly reordered by CDC.

PUBLIC RELATIONS SPECIALIST FOR U.S. MILITARY, LAUNCHED SOCIAL MEDIA CAMPAIGN. Managed Air Force Social Media account. Revamped Airman Magazine's Facebook page; developed social media strategy, emphasizing youthful, personal approach. Enabled military personnel to post unclassified cell phone photos and videos on Air Force social media websites: pictures of Airmen's Halloween party, imitating actors in famous movies, Air Force flyovers, astronauts training or eating at restaurants. Gauged and quantified community reaction to social media outlets to determine what stories people would react to. RESULT: Airman Magazine had 1,037 online fans when I took over the account. That number quickly tripled. Airman Magazine now has more than 5,000 Facebook fans, resulting in a greater potential audience for the Air Force's message.

SUBSTITUTE TEACHER, ON A CHALLENGING ASSIGNMENT. Was recruited to teach a high-level high school English class. The class had five previous teachers that year. The students felt the lessons were not consistent and their academic needs weren't being met. I finished the year with the students, teaching lessons about Edgar Allan Poe and Anne Frank. RESULT: Students felt the end of the year was a success. Many students personally thanked me at graduation for walking them through the end of the year.

Ph.D. STUDENT WITH ACADEMIC HONORS:

- Currently serve on two editorial boards (rare honor for a student)
- Invited to serve on Campbell Collaboration editorial board, as a reviewer for Campbell and Cochrane Collaborations, and as Managing Editor of Research on Social Work Practice
- Research Methodological Studies Award: competitive application, received $1,800
- Received Academic Leadership Award: given to 12 students across campus
- Received Graduate Student Leadership Award: given to 1 student across campus; recognizes strong leadership skills through peer mentoring, teaching, research, publishing, creative work, service, and/or participation in professional association activities

ENGLISH PROFESSOR, ON CREATIVELY DEVELOPING CURRICULUM FOR DIVERSE STUDENT BODY. Developed curriculum and taught course, Gender in the Humanities, to student body which largely had not had exposure to complex discussions or presentations of issues related to gender, race, and sexuality. Researched course-related materials, texts. Chose subject matter that cut across cultural boundaries for students from ethnically diverse region of Southern California. Conducted lectures, demonstrating ability to communicate orally. Projects included public service commercial on domestic violence, student-run conference on mentoring, and museum exhibit on racial and sexual stereotypes of Asian women. Students researched portrayals of Asian women in mainstream media and entertainment for exhibit.

FOUNDED CONSTRUCTION FIRM WITH ZERO OSHA VIOLATIONS. Founded and grew an agile, technologically-adept construction firm with up to 40 full time employees and $3M annual budget, with diverse mix of commercial, government, and military clients. RESULTS: Nine years of construction with zero OSHA violations. Seven years certified accident-free by the Commercial Contractors' Self-Insurance Agency.

CONSTRUCTION PROJECT MANAGER ON SIGNIFICANT HISTORIC PROJECTS. Plan, manage and oversee large, complex new construction, including historical renovation projects. Closely involved in initial and continuous design modifications for federally significant multi-million dollar historic projects. Regularly consulted with architects, engineers and historic preservation professionals. Ensured painstaking accuracy in restoration and major modernization concurrently updating the HVAC, plumbing and electrical.

Selected Project Management Highlights:

- 2006: Hired by General Contractor to remodel historic 1790 3-story property in XXX, VA with Civil War significance. Project completed with no added costs or delays despite near collapse of building due to foundation issues.
- 2010: Built US Marine Corps Battalion HQ, XXX, VA. $3.5M cost, 15,000 sq. ft. design-build project. Completed one month ahead of schedule and on budget.

SMALL BUSINESS OWNER CREATES START-UP BUSINESS PLAN. Developed and implemented business plan for new start-up real estate business. Initiated and negotiated diverse contract actions. Managed contracts, inspections, reports, disclosures, deadlines and closing activities. Executed contract terminations, processed transactions, resolved discrepancies, conflict and complaints. Oversaw contractor performance. Developed and fostered effective business relationships with 3,000+ leads in 3 years. RESULTS: Closed more than $76,000 in new contracts in first six months.

STEP FOUR
Find the Perfect Job Announcement

A Systematic Federal Job Search

You've done a lot of homework in Steps 1 through 3. Now it's finally time to start looking for vacancy announcements. Fortunately, most of your searching for federal job announcements will easily be done online. The Resume Builder Chart in Step 8 shows which websites and builders the major agencies currently use. This table should give you a starting point, but make sure to verify that the information for your agencies of interest is up-to-date.

To get started, set up your accounts and profiles on the websites serving the agencies you are targeting, such as:

- ✪ USAJOBS (www.usajobs.gov)
- ✪ Application Manager (www.applicationmanager.gov)
- ✪ AvueCentral (www.avuecentral.com)
- ✪ CPOL (www.cpol.army.mil)
- ✪ DONHR (https://chart.donhr.navy.mil)

When you create your profile(s), check that you will accept Term, Temporary, and Career Conditional positions. With a change in administration, many positions will be posted as term or temporary positions. These positions provide an opportunity for you to get into the federal government, and you can later apply for a status position. As a term or temporary employee, you will receive many of the same benefits as your full-time status counterparts.

Write down your vacancy announcement search plan and, if necessary, schedule it as a regular activity.

Strategy Tip

To save time, make sure to sign up for automatic search agents on websites such as USAJOBS to receive regular email announcements about job openings matching your search criteria.

How often you check the websites for new announcements depends in large part on how much time you have available to dedicate to your job search. In general, you should be prepared to check announcements at least weekly in order to ensure that you do not miss a potentially matching job announcement.

Here are some sample plans:

Plan 1 – USAJOBS Only

USAJOBS "All Search" weekly check

Set up and read automatic search agent emails

Plan 2 – More Comprehensive Search

USAJOBS "All Search" weekly check

Set up and read automatic search agent emails

Agency listings weekly check

Check other websites weekly, such as AvueCentral, Indeed (www.indeed.com), or Washington Post Jobs (or www.washingtonpost.com/wl/jobs/home).

Plan 3 – Focus on Army Positions

Search on CPOL (www.cpol.army.mil) – all of the Army positions are posted here

USAJOBS search weekly for positions other than Army

Set up and read automatic search agent emails on USAJOBS

Strategy Tip

Sometimes jobseekers will update a resume on USAJOBS when they are really applying for a job with the Army – which would be the CPOL site. Remember that if you are applying for an Army position, you will need to submit your resume to the Army resume builder and self-nominate at the Army's recruitment website, www.cpol.army.mil. If you want to apply for a Navy position, make sure to take the same steps on the Navy's website. If you want to apply for a position at the Department of the Interior, apply to USAJOBS and submit answers to questions at Application Manager.

Types of Job Announcements

Job Announcements with Specific Closing Dates

These announcements are for positions that are being recruited for specifically. Timing for response could be as little as several days or as long as several weeks.

Transportation Security Administration

Job Title: Program Assistant - SV-0344-E
Department: Department Of Homeland Security
Agency: Transportation Security Administration
Sub Agency: DHS-Transportation Security Administration
Job Announcement Number: LAX-11-366608

SALARY RANGE:	$37,260.00 - $55,959.00 /year
OPEN PERIOD:	Wednesday, June 08, 2011 to Tuesday, June 21, 2011
SERIES & GRADE:	SV-0344-E/E

Open Inventory – Standing Registers – Database Announcements

These announcements are continually being recruited for, or they anticipate a future need for candidates. The closing date could be far into the future or nonexistent. The names of qualified applicants are stored in a database, and HR will search the database when a supervisor requests a person meeting the job's requirements. Timing for filling jobs covered by this kind of announcement is unknown, so be prepared for a long wait.

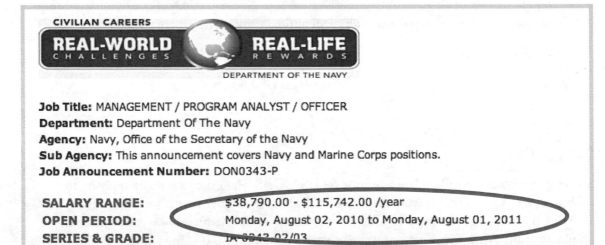

CIVILIAN CAREERS

REAL-WORLD CHALLENGES **REAL-LIFE** REWARDS

DEPARTMENT OF THE NAVY

Job Title: MANAGEMENT / PROGRAM ANALYST / OFFICER
Department: Department Of The Navy
Agency: Navy, Office of the Secretary of the Navy
Sub Agency: This announcement covers Navy and Marine Corps positions.
Job Announcement Number: DON0343-P

SALARY RANGE:	$38,790.00 - $115,742.00 /year
OPEN PERIOD:	Monday, August 02, 2010 to Monday, August 01, 2011
SERIES & GRADE:	IA-0343-02/03

Job Announcements with Cut-offs; Multiple / Rolling Deadlines

You might see an announcement with a closing date of three months from today and have cut-off dates in addition to the final deadline. The human resources specialists will not close the collection of resumes until the final deadline. They will check their resumes in the database at the cut-off dates, but they will wait until the end of the time period to review all resumes for consideration.

Federal Job Websites

USAJOBS
www.usajobs.gov

This is the Office of Personnel Management's main website for federal jobs. It is free of charge and very easy to use.

Quick Start: Search ALL JOBS

This is the No. 1 search strategy on USAJOBS, as recommended by OPM's USAJOBS' managers and website developer.

Quick Search Instructions:
- Go to USAJOBS (www.usajobs.gov).
- Click on SEARCH JOBS.
- You will see two fields: "What: (keywords)" and "Where: (U.S. city, state or zip code)."
- Type in your geographic preference in the "Where" field.
- Click on the "Search Jobs" button.
- USAJOBS will return a list of all the jobs in the area you specified.
- You can further refine your search to the appropriate salary or grade range in the upper right hand area under "Refine Your Results."

This search will present all of the job titles in this geographic area in your salary or grade range. You can review the job titles and duties to determine if the jobs are of interest to you. It is important to search for ALL JOBS, because federal job titles are not as straightforward as we would like, and they are prone to change as new job needs arise in agencies. If you limit your job search to a particular job title with which you are familiar, you may not learn about all of the job openings for which you are qualified—or even those that represent your particular field of interest. For instance, would you automatically think to search for Program Specialist or Management Analyst? Surprisingly, these popular government job titles mean many things. The range of program possibilities is phenomenal—environmental, food and nutrition, transportation, education, health, health insurance, and homeland security. You name it. The government probably has a program specialist or management analyst working on it! Sorting through the list of jobs will take time, but as you learn the job titles and functions, you will gradually be able to accurately target your job search, and it will likely save you time in the long run.

Set Up Search Agents in USAJOBS

You can create up to five search agents in USAJOBS to receive emails on a daily, weekly, or monthly basis with specific job titles, geographic region, and grade or salary. But beware: you should not rely only on this system completely. If you do use the ALL SEARCH as described above, there will be some job titles that will not come up with your search agent.

Strategy Tip
Do the ALL SEARCH on a weekly basis AND set up your job search agents as well.

Application Manager
www.applicationmanager.gov

Application Manager is provided by the Office of Personnel Management and powered by USA Staffing™, a tool to submit and track application packages. Application Manager, like a handful of other federal staffing systems, is integrated with USAJOBS to accept USAJOBS resumes. Application Manager "takes over" management of the application process once you leave USAJOBS. Application Manager presents any assessments you need to complete, collects any supporting documents that are required, and provides detailed feedback to applicants as the process goes forward. Some agencies will use Application Manager as their only recruitment system.

This website makes applying to multiple announcements easier by keeping on file all of your personal information, the documents you have submitted, and your responses to questionnaires. Application Manager will also help to ensure that your application package is complete.

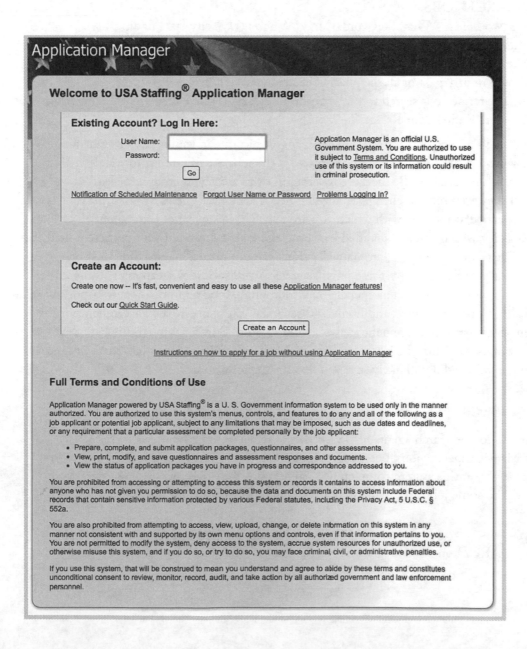

Avue Central Recruiting System

www.avuecentral.com

Avue Central is a competitor of USAJOBS. This system is developed and maintained by Avue Digital Services, a private industry company providing recruitment services for federal agencies. Avue Central services approximately 25 federal agencies with their resume builder, questionnaire, and essays. Agencies using Avue Central place their job announcements here as well as on USAJOBS. Avue Central is a free, easy-to-use website.

You can input your resume into their database with their resume builder and apply for jobs with any of their client agencies with a simple click. The search screen is simple to scroll through, with as many as 20 job announcements per screen.

Agencies and Organizations Using Avue Central

- Architect of the Capitol
- Carahsoft Technology Corporation
- Court Services and Offender Supervision Agency
- Department of Justice
- Drug Enforcement Administration
- Federal Air Marshal Service
- Fratelli Coalition Site
- International Leadership Foundation
- Library of Congress

- Millennium Challenge Corporation
- Office of Federal Housing Enterprise Oversight
- Peace Corps
- Securities and Exchange Commission
- Society of American Indian Government Employees
- US Agency for International Development
- USDA Forest Service
- United States Capitol Police
- Department of Agriculture

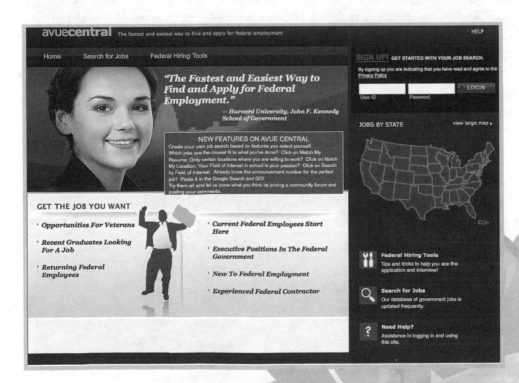

Resumix™ (U.S. Department of Defense)

Resumix is a keyword search system. The human resources specialist will search the database with five to seven critical keywords/skills/phrases taken from the vacancy announcements. A key difference between Resumix and the other automated hiring systems we have mentioned is that Resumix does not use your answers to job-specific questions to determine whether, and how well, you are qualified for a job. But like the other systems, it does require a Profile set-up with personnel questions to establish your account and to determine your eligibility for federal employment. After that, the focus is on the content of your resume.

Department of Defense agencies (including the military services for their civilian hiring) use Resumix™, a resume-driven system for Civilian Personnel Hiring and Management. NASA also uses Resumix in addition to the USAJOBS Resume Builder for resume collections. Several agencies are working on a new internal recruitment system that will eliminate Resumix, but as of this printing, the Resumix system is still in use.

NOTE: DOD Resumix will be eliminated within the next two years, and all applications for DOD Resumix will be recieved through USAJOBS. Navy CHART will be eliminated in the near future, and all applications will be received by USAJOBS and Application Manager.

Department of the Army Civilian Personnel (Resumix)
www.cpol.army.mil

Although the U.S. Army posts its civilian vacancies on the Army site AND the USAJOBS website, you MUST post your resume into the Army's resume builder. If you are interested in civilian positions with the U.S. Army, you might save time by going directly to the Army website to find the announcements and apply for the jobs.

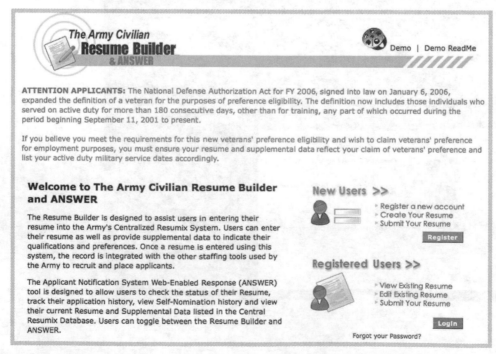

Department of the Navy Civilian Jobs (Resumix)
https://chart.donhr.navy.mil/

The U.S. Navy and Marine Corps have their own website on which you can post your resume. You may copy and paste your resume into their online resume builder, then search for announcements that match your qualifications. Click Search Jobs and then Search All Jobs to search for civilian job vacancies by geographic area, salary, or job title.

Internships with the Navy or Marines are also listed on this website. You MUST apply for jobs or internships through this system. The resume builder on this website is very simple and easy to complete.

NOTE: The Department of Navy announcements are not particularly descriptive. They may have "generic" job descriptions instead of specific "duties," like other announcements. These are "Open Inventory" or database announcements.

Jobseekers may not take these employment opportunities seriously because the closing dates for the jobs may be 2012. However, they are real jobs; HR staff will search for the best candidates when a supervisor has a position to fill.

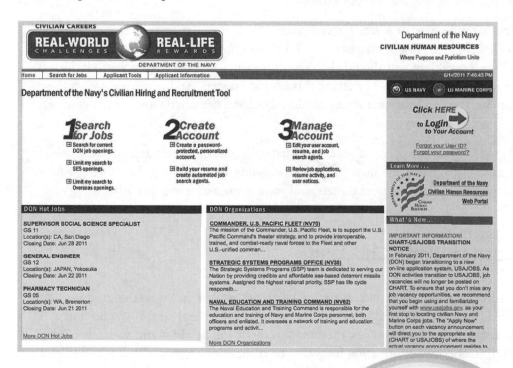

Strategy Tip

POTENTIAL BUILDER PITFALL! Sometimes a job applicant will forget they are applying to an Army announcement and will update their USAJOBS resume instead of their Army resume. The result is that you may not actually be applying for the Army announcement.

Agency Job Listing Websites

Most departments and agencies have their own job information websites or pages. They may also provide information to USAJOBS.

If you are focusing your job search on specific agencies, register at these agencies' websites and search for jobs within their listings. Frequently, agencies provide more information on their own websites about jobs and how to apply for them than they include in the announcements placed on USAJOBS. Individual agency websites also include their database registration pages for their on-line application forms.

Traditional vs. Nontraditional Civil Service

Size breeds complexity! The federal government comprises hundreds of separate organizations. Many of these organizations belong to the traditional civil service, and follow a common set of hiring rules. Others, however, lie outside the traditional civil service, and may have their own hiring policies. To complicate things even further, one agency may have different hiring policies within each department. If you are interested in working for any of these agencies, be sure to check the agencies' websites to learn about vacancies.

The fact that not all vacancies are located in one place is both a challenge and an opportunity for you. It is a challenge, because it suggests that you should not rely only on the USAJOBS site when you look for federal jobs, but should also consult websites of federal agencies for which you might want to work. You cannot lose by taking this additional step. And while you are on the agency-specific site, you can learn useful information about the agency, its mission, its culture, and its jobs.

Remember also to keep an eye open for other ways federal agencies recruit and advertise their openings. For example, agencies are increasingly participating in or running their own job fairs. They may recruit through school career centers, and some even use newspaper advertising.

Other Websites Worth Checking

Other websites that you may want to frequent are Washington Post (www.washingtonpost.com) and Indeed (www.indeed.com), which will sometimes list federal jobs. If you do find a federal announcement on these two sites, the announcement will be short and sweet. It might not contain all of the needed information for you to be competitive against those who have read the announcement on the www.usajobs.gov website, so try to see if you can locate the same announcement on USAJOBS.

Sample Agency Website: U.S. Department of Health & Human Services

U.S. Department of Health & Human Services

HHS.gov

Frequent Questions   A-Z Index

[Search box]   Search
○ This Site   ○ All HHS Sites

Email Updates ✉   Font Size ⊖ ⊕   Print 🖨   Download Reader ↧

| Home | About Us | HHS Secretary | News | Jobs | Grants/Funding | Families | Prevention | Diseases | Regulations | Preparedness |

HHS Home > Careers

Careers
Where Can I Work?
Find and Apply for Jobs
Pay & Benefits
Education & Training Programs
Student Programs
Opportunities for College Graduates
About Human Resources

HHS Careers

Do you need assistance discovering the right career? What about information on how to apply for Federal employment opportunities? Are you interested in learning about the benefits afforded to Federal employees? Then, HHS Careers is a one stop resource for all your employment needs!

The U.S. Department of Health and Human Services (HHS) is the government's principal agency for protecting the health and well-being of all Americans. This is a tremendous responsibility and requires HHS to employ individuals who are willing and able to respond to the call.

Why Should You Bring Your Career to HHS?

Are you looking for a challenge? A career dedicated to improving the health and well-being of all Americans? A career that can impact healthcare around the world? A career where you can do well by doing good?

Then come to HHS! The U.S. Department of Health and Human Services family of agencies improves the health and well-being of people here at home and around the world every single day.

Are you up to the challenge?

HHS employs individuals from diverse social and academic backgrounds into a full range of career fields and positions: doctors, nurses, biologists, social and physical scientists, economists, computer specialists, budget analysts, administrative and clerical specialists, and epidemiologists – to name a few. Are you someone who can assist us in accomplishing our mission? If so, we encourage you to apply!

This Page in Spanish

En Español

USA Jobs

USAJOBS
"WORKING FOR AMERICA"

Search and apply for Federal Jobs at www.USAJobs.gov.

Help Desk Contacts

📞   Careers Help Desk Contacts

HHS Home | Questions? | Contacting HHS | Accessibility | Privacy Policy | FOIA | Disclaimers | The White House | USA.gov | HHS Archive | Pandemic Flu | Viewers & Players
U.S. Department of Health & Human Services - 200 Independence Avenue, S.W. - Washington, D.C. 20201

Excepted Agencies

Excepted agencies do NOT necessarily list on USAJOBS. These agencies utilize some of the "nontraditional" hiring practices. These agencies may post their vacancies on USAJOBS, but you should also check their home pages when you are conducting your federal job search.

- Transportation Security Administration, Department of Homeland Security
- Federal Reserve System, Board of Governors
- Central Intelligence Agency
- Defense Intelligence Agency, Department of Defense
- Foreign Service, U.S. Department of State
- Federal Bureau of Investigation, Department of Justice
- Agency for International Development
- National Security Agency, Department of Defense
- National Imagery and Mapping Agency, Department of Defense
- U.S. Nuclear Regulatory Commission
- Postal Rate Commission
- Health Services and Research Administration, Department of Veterans Affairs (physicians, nurses, and allied medical personnel)
- Judicial Branch
- Legislative Branch (including the Government Accountability Office)

Government Corporations, such as:
- U. S. Postal Service
- Tennessee Valley Authority
- The Virgin Islands Corporation

Public International Organizations:
- International Monetary Fund
- Pan American Health Organization
- United Nations Children's Fund
- United Nations Development Program
- United Nations Institute
- United Nations Population Fund
- United Nations Secretariat
- World Bank, IFC and MIGA

Troutman Method Lesson 2:
Interpreting a Vacancy Announcement

The most important point that you need to take away from this step is to read the vacancy announcement very carefully. You not only need to comply with the requirements of the vacancy announcement perfectly, you also need to use keywords from the announcement to prepare a successful application package.

Title of Job, Grade, and Salary

Be sure the job is right for you. Some job titles in government are unusual and not typically recognized in the employment world. However, they might be just right for you. For instance:

- Budget Analyst, GS-12/13, DE; Salary: $69,764 to $107,854; Executive Office of the President, 1 Vacancy, Washington, DC; Position Information: Career/Career Conditional Position in Competitive Service; Permanent Position

- Administrative Assistant, GS-0303-09/09; Promotion Potential to GS-9; Salary: $50,285 to $65,276; Department of Justice, U.S. Attorneys, Executive Office & Office of U.S. Attorneys, Eastern District of New York; Full-time Permanent Career or Career-Conditional Appointment in the Competitive Service

- Energy Management Specialist, GS-1102-9/12; Promotion Potential to GS-12; Salary: $36,671 to $84,559; Department of Defense, Defense Logistics Agency, Ft. Belvoir, Fairfax, VA; Full-time Career/Career Conditional

- Contract Specialist, GS-1102-9/12; Promotion potential to GS-12; U.S. Secret Service, Department of Homeland Security

Strategy Tip

Read the vacancy announcement very carefully, paying close attention to these sections: Duties; Qualifications; Knowledge, Skills and Abilities; Questionnaires; and How to Apply.

Closing Date

Be aware that applications submitted after the closing date will NOT be considered. Therefore, check the job announcement listings at least weekly so that you will have enough time to submit your applications. If the closing date says "Open Continuously," "Inventory Building," or has a closing date that is far off in the future, then the organization is using this announcement to build an inventory of future job candidates. Names of qualified applicants will be placed in a database for future (and also, possibly, current) job openings. Such announcements represent many jobs that the agency expects to open up at any time.

Who Can Apply

What does "Open to Anyone With or Without Status" mean? If the announcement says "Open to Anyone," then you can apply. "Status" refers to current federal employees and former employees whose length of previous federal employment and type of appointment qualify them for reinstatement. NOTE: Most federal civil service jobs require U.S. citizenship, but jobs in other federal systems (such as the Postal Service, National Institutes of Health, and other agencies) may not. If you are not a U.S. citizen, read this part of the announcement carefully.

In USAJOBS, when you search for jobs, you can specify your applicant elibility on your search results page by clicking on the radio button for either:

✪ "Only Public Jobs Open To ALL U.S. Citizens" or

✪ "ALL Jobs (Public and Status)"

Agency/Office

The office where the job is located is very important. Researching and understanding the office mission could help you write a more targeted resume. The office title could also provide clues about the mission of the job, such as Information Technology, Legal Services, Policy and Planning, or Equal Employment Opportunity (EEO).

Location/Duty Station

Make sure you are willing to work in the geographic location of the position you are seeking. When hiring new employees, federal agencies must accept applications regardless of where the applicant lives. (For example, an agency must accept an application from a person living in Florida who seeks a job in Alaska). However, the agency may refuse to pay moving and relocation expenses. Read the announcement carefully to find out what your obligations are.

Knowledge, Skills, and Abilities (KSAs or Competencies)

Read the announcement carefully to see if KSA narratives will be required written on separate sheets of paper, or if the KSAs can be described in the text of your resume. (See Step 7 for more instruction on KSA writing.)

Duties

Always read the duties carefully because the title of the position may not accurately reflect the duties of the job. Pay close attention to the language in the announcement discussing the **one year specialized experience**. The HR Specialist will be looking for your one year specialized experience in areas of work similar to the performance level of the announcement.

Qualifications and One Year Specialized Experience

One year of specialized experience means that you have one year of experience that is specialized in this work and at this level. Read the required qualifications to determine if you have the generalized and specialized experience, or the education that can substitute for it. If the announcement uses the term "one year," it means 52 weeks, 40 hours per week. Relevant experience gained from part-time jobs can be combined to determine how much job-related experience you have. If the hours combine to make one year of specialized experience, then you can be credited with that year.

For many jobs, qualifications are expressed in terms of experience or education, or combinations of the two. Possession of a Bachelor's Degree is often enough to qualify someone for an entry-level (GS-5 or sometimes GS-7) job in many professional or administrative occupations.

For career changers returning to college for another degree, you may qualify for your new career as a GS-5, 7, or 9 based on your education alone. You will probably have to move back in your earnings, but with potential to move ahead in your new career.

How to Apply

Follow all of the directions very carefully. Read the instructions to determine what to send with your application and which resume format to use. Sometimes this is not clear. While most agencies now use an online application system that takes you step-by-step through the application process, many still do not. The burden is squarely on the applicant to submit a complete, accurate application in a timely manner. If you are going to take the time to apply for a federal job, be sure you submit a complete application! See Step 8 for more details on applying for jobs.

Questionnaires, Core Questions, Vacancy-Specific Questions, and Job-Specific Questions

Be aware that submitting your resume may just be part one of your application. Many announcements will require you to fill out additional questions, known as the self-assessment questionnaire, as part of your application. You will be rating your skill level in the questions. The question format will be multiple choice, yes/no, true/false, check all that apply, and essay questions. You will be graded on your answers – and the grade will determine your score for your application. A human resources specialist gave this instruction to a class at the Environmental Protection Agency: "Give yourself the most credit that you can when answering the questions." You will learn more about Questionnaires in Step 7.

Resume Submission Page in USAJOBS

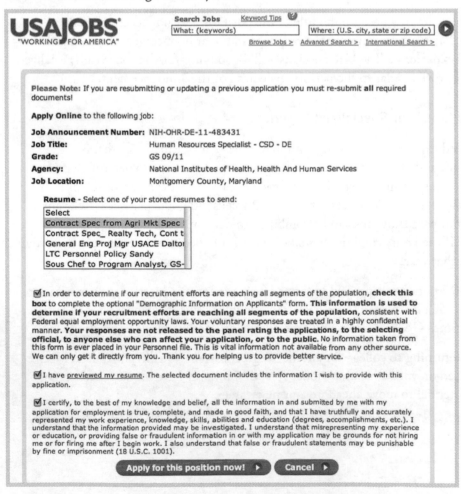

Bridge Page to Application Manager

Application Manager

Welcome to USA Staffing® Application Manager!

If you have already created an Application Manager account, please log in on the next page.

If this is the first time USAJOBS has sent you to Application Manager, to continue the job application process, you will need to create an account.

Application Manager, https://ApplicationManager.gov, is a completely separate system that some agencies use to collect applications online; it is not a part of http://www.USAJOBS.gov. This means you need a separate account with Application Manager to continue the online application process. In Application Manager you will answer detailed job-specific questions that go beyond what you have done in USAJOBS, and you can attach documents to your application package, including your USAJOBS résumé. See the Application Manager Quick Start Guide for an overview.

Continue

Sample Assessment Questionnaire Page in Application Manager

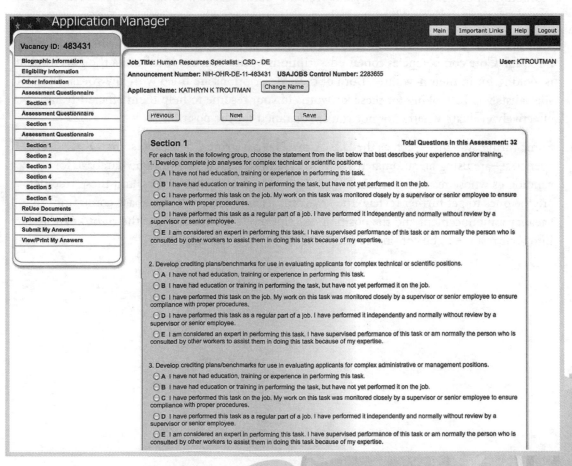

Application Manager

Main | Important Links | Help | Logout

Vacancy ID: 483431

Biographic Information
Eligibility Information
Other Information
Assessment Questionnaire
  Section 1
Assessment Questionnaire
  Section 1
Assessment Questionnaire
  Section 1
  Section 2
  Section 3
  Section 4
  Section 5
  Section 6
ReUse Documents
Upload Documents
Submit My Answers
View/Print My Answers

Job Title: Human Resources Specialist - CSD - DE
Announcement Number: NIH-OHR-DE-11-483431 **USAJOBS Control Number:** 2283655
Applicant Name: KATHRYN K TROUTMAN   Change Name

User: KTROUTMAN

Previous | Next | Save

Section 1
Total Questions in this Assessment: 32

For each task in the following group, choose the statement from the list below that best describes your experience and/or training.

1. Develop complete job analyses for complex technical or scientific positions.
- A I have not had education, training or experience in performing this task.
- B I have had education or training in performing the task, but have not yet performed it on the job.
- C I have performed this task on the job. My work on this task was monitored closely by a supervisor or senior employee to ensure compliance with proper procedures.
- D I have performed this task as a regular part of a job. I have performed it independently and normally without review by a supervisor or senior employee.
- E I am considered an expert in performing this task. I have supervised performance of this task or am normally the person who is consulted by other workers to assist them in doing this task because of my expertise.

2. Develop crediting plans/benchmarks for use in evaluating applicants for complex technical or scientific positions.
- A I have not had education, training or experience in performing this task.
- B I have had education or training in performing the task, but have not yet performed it on the job.
- C I have performed this task on the job. My work on this task was monitored closely by a supervisor or senior employee to ensure compliance with proper procedures.
- D I have performed this task as a regular part of a job. I have performed it independently and normally without review by a supervisor or senior employee.
- E I am considered an expert in performing this task. I have supervised performance of this task or am normally the person who is consulted by other workers to assist them in doing this task because of my expertise.

3. Develop crediting plans/benchmarks for use in evaluating applicants for complex administrative or management positions.
- A I have not had education, training or experience in performing this task.
- B I have had education or training in performing the task, but have not yet performed it on the job.
- C I have performed this task on the job. My work on this task was monitored closely by a supervisor or senior employee to ensure compliance with proper procedures.
- D I have performed this task as a regular part of a job. I have performed it independently and normally without review by a supervisor or senior employee.
- E I am considered an expert in performing this task. I have supervised performance of this task or am normally the person who is consulted by other workers to assist them in doing this task because of my expertise.

STEP Five
Identify Your Keywords

Why Keywords Are Important

1. If you look around, you will find keywords in just about everything: advertisements, promotions, book covers, websites, and even on your cereal box. In today's "quick read," iPod, text messaging, and sound bite world, keywords represent who you are.

2. The vacancy announcement contains a technical description of the position you hope to be hired for. Core competencies contain descriptions of the "value-added" traits the government is looking for in their new hires. Both of these descriptions are filled with keywords. The HR specialists will be looking for these keywords in your resume to help them efficiently and effectively evaluate whether or not you are qualified for the position.

3. Some hiring systems—such as the U.S. Army, Navy, Marine Corps, and some DOD agencies—are using an automated keyword system to search their resume database for candidates whose resumes contain five to eight pre-identified keywords, and these resumes are the ones to get further review. The keywords used to search the database come from the vacancy announcement and the position description. It is critical to get the right keywords into your resume to be considered for positions in these hiring systems.

Troutman Method Lesson 3:
Finding Keywords in the Vacancy Announcement

Once you have found a promising vacancy announcement, it is time to analyze the announcement for keywords.

The simple steps outlined here have been successfully used by thousands of federal job applicants to break the vacancy announcement code.

1. Save the vacancy announcement as an html file.

2. You will be reviewing these sections from the announcement for keywords:
    - ✪ Duties
    - ✪ Qualifications
    - ✪ Specialized Experience
    - ✪ Knowledge, Skills, and Abilities
    - ✪ Questionnaires
    - ✪ Agency or organization mission

3. Copy and paste these sections from the announcement into a word processing program such as Word or WordPerfect.

4. Enlarge the type to 14 or 16 points to make the print more readable.

5. Separate each sentence by increasing the line spacing for the entire document.

6. Delete useless words such as "the incumbent will" or "duties will encompass a variety of tasks including."

7. Underline or highlight keywords and skills that are significant to the position, such as "identifying deficiencies in human performance" and "recommending changes for correction."

Example: John Wallstone

To show you how to use the techniques we teach in this book, we chose to feature a real life example: John Wallstone (real person, fictitious name). John was a sous chef seeking a federal job as a Program Analyst at FEMA. His successful career change resume was also used in the second edition and inspired thousands of jobseekers. John landed a GS-11 Program Analyst position at FEMA with the techniques and the resume that you will see in this book. Since then, John has twice been promoted. Below, see how John highlighted the key skills in this job announcement.

Target Announcement: Program Analyst, GS 9/11/12

Duties for this position may include all or part of the following:

Conducts needs assessment surveys using complex methods for assigned program(s). Collects, analyzes, and maintains data required to manage assigned programs (i.e. historical, statistical, etc). Researches and **investigates best practices** for applications to organization/agency programs or operations. Incumbent conducts studies of efficiency and productivity. Incumbent conducts studies and **analysis of operations, procedures and policies,** and **analyzes staff strengths and weaknesses**, to determine if more efficient or cost effective methods/practices can be achieved or if **customer satisfaction** can be improved.

Identifies resources required to support varied levels of program operations. **Compiles budget information** and **performs cost and price comparative analysis** to determine fiscal resources for implementing changes in pricing and practices.

Develops management and/or program evaluation plans, procedures, and methodology. Recommends changes or improvements to **achieve the highest efficiency** in programs and **ensures efficient business processes. Manages operations** by **directing staff** to implement recommended changes. **Creates a timeline of implementation** and monitors the development of and evaluates the execution of project(s) and program(s). Incumbent will **develop new pricing and cost accounting procedures** based on analysis of findings. **Oversees vendor contracts** to **ensure efficiency, security, and reduce waste.**

John's Keyword List

Next, pull out the highlighted words and create a list of keywords. Eliminate duplication and unnecessary words (such as "a" and "the") and use active verbs to create the most succinct, but complete, list that you can. You can also reorder the list alphabetically or group them according to categories depending on which format is easier for you to use.

Announcement Keywords (listed alphabetically)

- ✪ Achieve highest efficiency
- ✪ Analyze operations, procedures, and policies
- ✪ Analyze staff strengths/weaknesses
- ✪ Best practices
- ✪ Compile budget information
- ✪ Conduct needs assessment surveys
- ✪ Create project timeline
- ✪ Customer satisfaction
- ✪ Develop pricing and cost accounting procedures
- ✪ Develop pricing and marketing information
- ✪ Direct staff
- ✪ Ensure efficiency, security, and reduce waste
- ✪ Ensure efficient business processes
- ✪ Manage operations
- ✪ Oversee vendor contracts
- ✪ Perform cost and price comparative analysis
- ✪ Recommend and implement changes

Announcement Keywords (grouped by category)

- ✪ Achieve highest efficiency
- ✪ Ensure efficiency, security, and reduce waste
- ✪ Ensure efficient business processes
- ✪ Best practices
- ✪ Customer satisfaction

- ✪ Conduct needs assessment surveys
- ✪ Analyze operations, procedures, and policies
- ✪ Analyze staff strengths/weaknesses
- ✪ Perform cost and price comparative analysis
- ✪ Compile budget information

- ✪ Recommend and implement changes
- ✪ Develop pricing and cost accounting procedures
- ✪ Develop pricing and marketing information
- ✪ Direct staff
- ✪ Create project timeline
- ✪ Manage operations
- ✪ Oversee vendor contracts

More Samples of Keyword Lists

These samples contain actual keyword lists from true federal job seeking stories.

Sample 1: Benjamin Gaston
Target Position: Administration / Program Management, GS-0343

Announcement: Duties section

The selectee will serve as a **Management and Program Analyst** and will be responsible for performing a wide range of highly complex duties and for providing **technical guidance** and advice. Duties include but are not limited to the following: developing, administering, coordinating, and **analyzing accountability** and **management programs, identifying problems, recommending solutions, and monitoring progress**; preparing reports and **studies on accountability** and **management activities** for internal and external purposes; responding to **external accountability** and **management evaluations** or studies organized by the Office of Management and Budget (OMB), Office of Inspector General (OIG), Government Accountability Office (GAO), National Archives and Records Administration (NARA), and other oversight agencies.

Specialized experience is experience that equipped the applicant with the knowledge, skills, and abilities to perform successfully the duties of the position, and that is typically in or related to **research and analytical studies**.

Announcement Keywords

- Accountability
- Analytical studies
- Develop and administer programs
- Identify problems
- Internal and external purposes
- Management activities
- Management and Program Analyst
- Monitor progress
- Prepare reports and studies
- Recommend solutions
- Research
- Technical guidance and advice

Sample 2: Barbara Kelly
Target Position: Accounting and Budget Group, GS-0500

Announcement: Duties and Specialized Experience sections

The incumbent will primarily **examine** insured depository institutions. The incumbent will travel within the AOR to visit institutions to **identify** all **factors** and **causes, unsafe and unsound practices,** and **violations of laws and regulations,** which have affected or may affect the **condition and soundness of the institutions.** This position involves **analyzing and classifying loans, liabilities and capital; reviewing lending practices for compliance with regulations** such as **Check 21, Fair and Accurate Credit Transactions Act, and Privacy of Consumer Information.** Meets with **insured depository institution** officials and/or boards of directors to discuss **findings of examination, corrective programs,** and commitments for correction of deficiencies. Develops **recommendations for correction of weaknesses or deficiencies.** Evaluates and **prepares written reports.**

Announcement Keywords

- ✪ Analyzing and classifying loans
- ✪ Compliance with Check 21
- ✪ Condition and soundness of institutions
- ✪ Correction for weaknesses
- ✪ Corrective programs
- ✪ Deficiencies
- ✪ Depository institution
- ✪ Examine insured depository institutions
- ✪ Fair and Accurate Credit Transactions Act
- ✪ Findings of examination
- ✪ Identify factors and causes
- ✪ Liabilities and capital
- ✪ Prepare written reports
- ✪ Reviewing lending practices
- ✪ Unsafe and unsound practices
- ✪ Violations of law and regulations

What Are Core Competencies?

Consider this scenario: what if you were as qualified as another job applicant from a technical standpoint? How would the hiring officials decide which one of you to select for the job?

Many jobseekers know to list their technical skills in their resume but neglect to list their "soft skills." These soft skills are your core competencies. To stand out above your competition, you must demonstrate your core competencies and show that you can offer something to the organization above and beyond your technical skills. You will, of course, have to be qualified with the right education and generalized or specialized experience, but these core competencies could make the difference in helping you become the best-qualified applicant among your peers.

Therefore, core competencies are another important source for keywords to include in your federal resume.

How to Use Core Competencies in Your Resume

Core competencies for a particular job opening may be found in the vacancy announcement, agency mission statement, program description, career descriptions on the agency's website, and sometimes in the classification standard for the position (found at http://www.opm.gov/fedclass/html/gsseries.asp).

Review these documents and ask yourself whether the text gives you clues as to the type of person the organization is looking to hire. For example, is customer service or flexibility/adaptability more important for the particular position or organization?

In this step, review the documents listed above and identify at least five to ten competencies that you can demonstrate in your past accomplishments. Add these competencies to your resume in the Work Experience descriptions for a stronger federal resume!

Veterans Administration Example

This step features the Veterans Administration set of core competencies developed by a group of human resource and organizational development specialists in New York. This list will give you a good starting point for identifying the major core competencies that most agencies are looking for in job applicants. Include statements about your core competencies in your resume, such as in the profile statement. Example: "Recognized for interpersonal skills with customers and coworkers."

Creative Thinking

- Appreciates new ideas and approaches
- Thinks and acts innovatively
- Looks beyond current reality and the "status quo"
- Demonstrates willingness to take risks
- Challenges assumptions
- Solves problems creatively
- Demonstrates resourcefulness
- Fosters creative thinking in others
- Allows and encourages employees to take risks
- Identifies opportunities for new projects and acts on them
- Rewards risk-taking and non-successes and values what was learned

Systems Thinking

- Understands the complexities of VA healthcare and how it is delivered
- Appreciates the consequences of specific actions on other parts of the system
- Thinks in context
- Knows how one's role relates to others in the organization
- Demonstrates awareness of the purpose, process, procedures, and outcomes of one's work
- Consistently focuses on the core business of the organization
- Asks questions that help others to think in a broader context
- Encourages and rewards collaboration

Technical Skills

- Displays knowledge and skills necessary to perform assigned duties
- Understands processes, procedures, standards, methods, and technologies related to assignment
- Demonstrates functional and technical literacy
- Participates in measuring outcomes of work
- Keeps current on new developments in field of expertise
- Effectively uses available technology (voice mail, automation, software, etc.)

Interpersonal Effectiveness

- Builds and sustains positive relationships
- Handles conflicts and negotiations effectively
- Earns trust and holds respect
- Collaborates and works well with others
- Shows sensitivity and compassion for others
- Encourages shared decision making
- Recognizes and uses ideas of others
- Communicates clearly, both orally and in writing
- Listens actively to others
- Honors commitments and promises

Customer Service

- Understands that customer service is essential to achieving the VA mission
- Models commitment to customer service
- Understands and meets the needs of internal customers
- Manages customer complaints and concerns effectively and promptly
- Designs work processes and systems that are responsive to customers
- Ensures that daily work and the VA's strategic direction are customer-centered
- Uses customer feedback data in planning and providing products and services
- Encourages and empowers subordinates to meet or exceed customer needs and expectations
- Identifies and rewards behaviors that enhance customer satisfaction

Flexibility/Adaptability

- Responds appropriately to new or changing situations
- Handles multiple inputs and tasks simultaneously
- Seeks and welcomes others' ideas
- Works well with all levels and types of people
- Accommodates new situations and realities
- Remains calm in high-pressure situations
- Makes the most of limited resources
- Demonstrates resilience in the face of setbacks
- Understands change management

Core Competencies: John Wallstone

Earlier in this chapter, we identified keywords from the announcement that John Wallstone applied to. As you may recall, John applied for a program analyst position at FEMA. Because John is seeking to make an obvious career change, he will need to demonstrate that he has transferable skills to the new position. Often for career change situations, it is the "soft skills" or the core competencies that are the transferable skills.

Studying the announcement for core competency language, we deduce that John should also include some keywords in his federal resume around these core competencies:

- ✪ **Information Management:** This is actually a technical skill that is implied in the vacancy announcement but not explicitly stated. The announcement contains many information-related duties, such conducting surveys, analysis, budget information, and program applications, and a person who could fulfill these duties must have some background or skill in information management.

- ✪ **Customer Service:** FEMA's mission at the time of John's application was "to reduce the loss of life and property and protect the Nation from all hazards, including natural disasters, acts of terrorism, and other man-made disasters, by leading and supporting the Nation in a risk-based, comprehensive emergency management system of preparedness, protection, response, recovery, and mitigation." According to this mission, FEMA provides a service to our country, so for FEMA and other agencies providing a service to the American public, customer service is often an important core competency to demonstrate.

- ✪ **Communications:** The new hire will be responsible for directing staff to implement changes, and this level of front line management will always require communication skills or interpersonal effectiveness.

Senior Executive Service Executive Core Qualifications

The Senior Executive Service Executive Core Qualifications statements (SEC ECQs) are mandatory for Senior Executive Service positions. Candidates for SES positions will be writing two pages of narratives for each of the five ECQs. Each ECQ will include two or three of your top accomplishments that demonstrate the ECQ and the definitions. These ECQs are very important for positions that are GS-9 and above. They are not mandator, but could prove to support your qualifications and experience.

Executive Core Qualifications (ECQs)

If you would like to apply for a Senior Executive Service position in government, you will have to write the five ECQs as part of your application. The best way to begin writing the ECQs is to write your Top Ten List of Accomplishments.

The Top Ten List of Executive Accomplishments can then be mapped into the five ECQs defined on the next page. You can find more details and examples of how to write ECQs at http://www.opm.gov/ses/recruitment/ecq.asp.

Senior Executive Service (SES)

The SES administers public programs at the top levels of the federal government. Positions are primarily managerial and supervisory. The SES is a tiered system in which salary is linked to individual performance, not position. Basic annual salaries range from $119,554 to $179,700, not including locality pay. Some positions include additional recruitment incentives. In setting pay rates, agencies consider such factors as qualifications, performance, duties, and responsibilities of the position, and private sector pay.

Total compensation (including salary, cash awards for top performance, relocation, recruitment, or retention allowances) may not exceed the pay for Executive Level I ($199,700 in 2011).

More information about SES can be found at https://www.opm.gov/ses.

For more help with your SES application, get our new release, *The New SES Application* by Kathryn Troutman and Diane Hudson Burns. Based on many years' experience in writing and teaching people to successfully apply for SES positions, this invaluable guide also includes the latest information about the new five-page executive federal resume. Order at www. resume-place.com.

Leading Change	Leading People	Results Driven	Business Acumen	Building Coalitions
Definitions				
This core qualification involves the ability to bring about strategic change, both within and outside the organization, to meet organizational goals. Inherent to this ECQ is the ability to establish an organizational vision and to implement it in a continuously changing environment.	This core qualification involves the ability to lead people toward meeting the organization's vision, mission, and goals. Inherent to this ECQ is the ability to provide an inclusive workplace that fosters the development of others, facilitates cooperation and teamwork, and supports constructive resolution of conflicts.	This core qualification involves the ability to meet organizational goals and customer expectations. Inherent to this ECQ is the ability to make decisions that produce high-quality results by applying technical knowledge, analyzing problems, and calculating risks.	This core qualification involves the ability to manage human, financial, and information resources strategically.	This core qualification involves the ability to build coalitions internally and with other federal agencies, state and local governments, nonprofit and private sector organizations, foreign governments, or international organizations to achieve common goals.
Leadership Competencies				
Creativity and Innovation	Conflict Management	Accountability	Financial Management	Partnering
External Awareness	Leveraging Diversity	Customer Service	Human Capital Management	Political Savvy
Flexibility	Developing Others	Decisiveness	Technology Management	Influencing/ Negotiating
Resilience	Team Building	Entrepre-neurship		
Strategic Thinking		Problem Solving		
Vision		Technical Credibility		

STEP SIX
Master the Federal Resume

Since the Last Edition...

Some aspects of federal resume writing have changed over the past year. Take note:

The resume is everything. Now that separate KSA narratives are mostly eliminated, the resume is the entire written application. You simply must get it right to be selected. Follow our proven formula!

KSAs are now included in the resume. The new requirement for many announcements is that you will need to add mini-KSA accomplishments into the text of the resume. You can see an example of how this is done in the sample federal resume in this step. In Step 7, we will explain more about KSAs in the resume.

Got a bucket? The latest new fad in human resources terms is, well, buckets. This is not a new feature in federal resumes, but an old one with a new name. Buckets are, quite simply, the critical skills listed in the vacancy announcement that applicants must show they have. On average, there are about five to seven buckets for each announcement. Each bucket has a number of keywords associated with it that you can find in the vacancy announcement in the duties, qualifications, KSAs, or questionnaire sections. So don't just get one bucket; you need them all in your resume, and we have found the easiest way to do that is to use one ALL CAPS Outline Format heading for each bucket. One HR specialist said this to me: "I can easily see the buckets of skills with the all cap headings. The accomplishments demonstrate their experience in each bucket area."

Here are some comments about federal resumes that are not new but are still critical:

Do you have the One Year Specialized Experience? This is a very simple, but sometimes overlooked, requirement. Make sure the HR specialist can find your all-important work experience to qualify for the job. HR specialists will first look at the dates (month and year), titles of positions, and salaries to determine if the level of your experience is equal to the position they are advertising. If your resume does not immediately demonstrate your One Year Specialized Experience qualification in these sections, then make sure the other sections of your resume tell clearly how you meet this requirement.

Your resume must match your questionnaire answers. The applicants whose questionnaires are scored in the top category receive the distinction of getting their resumes reviewed to ensure that the experience stated in the questionnaire is valid. This language came from an actual vacancy announcement: "In describing your experience, please be clear and specific. We may not make assumptions regarding your experience. If your resume does not support your questionnaire answers, we will not allow credit for your response(s)." Before you submit your final application for a position, go back and make sure that your resume supports your questionnaire answers.

Federal vs. Private Industry Resume

Private Industry

- One or two pages in length
- Keywords are desirable
- Fewer details in work descriptions
- No social security number, supervisors, or salaries given
- Focused on the mission of the business
- Profit motivated
- Customer service for customers who buy products
- Provides a product or service
- Creative, graphic, functional formats are okay
- Accomplishments are great
- Emphasis on ten years of experience
- More succinct writing style
- Honors, awards, and recognitions are important

Federal Resume

- Three to five pages is acceptable
- Keywords are needed
- More details for work descriptions to demonstrate your qualifications for a job
- Include SSN, supervisors' names, and salaries
- Focused on the mission of the agency, programs, and services
- Grant and budget motivated
- Customer service for millions of people, as well as internal customers
- Provides a program or service
- Chronological, traditional format
- Accomplishments are great
- Emphasis on ten years of experience
- Concise, yet informative content
- Honors, awards, and recognitions are more important

Checklist: Documents You Need to Write Your Federal Resume

Before you sit down to write your resume, it is very helpful to first collect into one place all of the background information you will need for your writing. Here is a list of items that you will need:

- Target vacancy announcements
- Other vacancy announcements for similar jobs
- Agency website, including program descriptions and mission language
- Classification Standards of desired positions (available at www.opm.gov)
- Your previous resume
- Position Descriptions
- Evaluations
- Private industry job websites

Troutman Method Lesson 4:
Create Your Federal Resume in the Outline Format

This lesson is the most important one in this book. We will focus on the hardest task in resume writing: drafting the heart of your resume, the work experience section. We will take your content, put it into the outline format, and target it toward the vacancy announcement. Take this lesson very seriously! Still not sure why? Read the myths and fear factors below.

Debunking the Myth

Many people think that the USAJOBS resumes are scanned by computers and artificial intelligence. This is NOT true. The USAJOBS resume system is a "human-read" system. Make your resume easy to scan and read for human resources specialists by using ALL CAP headings which clearly show that you are qualified for the position.

Debunking the Fear Factors/Reasons for Rejection

HR specialists complain that most federal resumes are hard to read or are too short. Most resumes do not demonstrate the qualifications for the position. Or, it is hard for the HR specialist to find the One Year Specialized Experience. The resumes include few or no accomplishments, do not show the relevant skills or keywords, and are not targeted toward a federal vacancy announcement. These resumes will not result in getting referred to any supervisor for futher consideration. If you want to eliminate this fear factor, follow the techniques in this step!

Features and benefits of the Outline Format:

- Headings include **keywords** from the vacancy announcement.
- Headings are in ALL CAPS for easy reading.
- Each paragraph in the Work Experience blocks represents a skill set.
- Each paragraph could also represent the KSAs that could be listed in the announcement.
- Paragraph length should be eight to ten lines at most.
- Separate Duties from Accomplishments.
- The format is easy to read and looks great in resume builders.
- Updates are easy—just edit and change the HEADLINES with new keywords.

Building Your Outline for the Work Experience Section

We are going to continue with John Wallstone's example, which we began in Step 5. As you may recall, John was a sous chef seeking a federal job as a program analyst.

This case study is a superb example of how it is possible to translate one career into another by analyzing and matching the keywords. Check out the keyword crosswalk from kitchen operations to program analyst.

Create Your Keyword Lists

It's interesting to compare the keywords from your current resume to the keywords for your target announcement. You will be amazed at the differences. When writing a federal resume, you must think forward—toward the skills required for the position—not backwards toward your past set of skills.

✪ Keywords from your previous resume (BEFORE resume keywords)

✪ Keywords from the target vacancy announcement (announcement keywords)

In Step 5, we showed you how John created his list of announcement keywords. We also explained a few core competencies that should be demonstrated in John's resume as well, and these are included in the announcement keyword list. Below on the left is a list of BEFORE resume keywords that we have created from John's private industry resume. Compare the two lists of keywords below.

Before Resume Keywords	Announcement Keywords
Catered events	Achieve highest efficiency
Cost control measures	Ensure efficiency, security, and reduce waste
Customer service agent	Ensure efficient business processes
Designed and directed production	Best practices
Executive Dining Room	Customer satisfaction
Food operations	Conduct needs assessment surveys
Implement sanitation programs	Analyze operations, procedures, and policies
Just in time inventory systems	Analyze staff strengths/weaknesses
Lead production teams	Perform cost and price comparative analysis
Maintained repeat customer clients	Compile budget information
Menu planning	Recommend and implement changes
New catering sales	Develop pricing and cost accounting procedures
Personal needs of first family	Develop pricing and marketing information
Petty cash funds	Direct staff
Promote safe food handling	Create project timeline
Purchasing, quality, and cost recommendations	Manage operations
Quality assurance	Oversee vendor contracts
Supervised staff	Information management
Updated computer technology	Customer service
Vending operations	Communication

Keyword Match—The Buckets

Next, we will perform a cross walk, or match, between the two keyword lists in an effort to come up with five to ten major groupings of keyword from both lists. One way to do this is shown below.

Manage operations
- Food operations
- Executive Dining Room
- Menu planning
- Achieve highest efficiency
- Best practices
- Analyze operations, procedures, and policies

Manage projects
- Catered events
- Conduct needs assessment surveys
- Create project timeline
- Analyze staff strengths/weaknesses

Manage supply
- Oversee vendor contracts
- Vending operations
- Just in time inventory systems
- Perform cost and price comparative analysis

Budget
- Develop pricing and cost accounting procedures
- Perform cost and price comparative analysis
- Develop pricing and marketing information
- Compile budget information
- Petty cash funds

Manage staff
- Direct staff
- Communication
- Lead production teams

Edit the Categories into Outline Headers

Looking at John's work experience, it became clear that John spent most of his time managing people, events, budgets, supply, etc. John's experience in managing is exactly what the hiring officials are looking for in this announcement. So in the end, we highlighted his management skills in the outline headings that we came up with. We also included the core competencies in the final list of outline headings because, as we mentioned in Step 5, these core competencies include many of the transferable skills for career change resumes.

Again, aim to create five to ten headings for the outline of your federal resume.

Here are the final outline headings we identified for John:

Before Resume Keywords	Announcement Keywords	Outline Headings
Catered events	Achieve highest efficiency	Operations Management
Cost control measures	Ensure efficiency, security, and reduce waste	Project Management
Customer service agent	Ensure efficient business processes	Supervisor / Team Lead
Designed and directed production	Best practices	Customer Servies
Executive Dining Room	Customer satisfaction	Supply Management
Food operations	Conduct needs assessment surveys	Budgeting / Funds Management
Implement sanitation programs	Analyze operations, procedures, and policies	Logistics Management
Just in time inventory systems	Analyze staff strengths/weaknesses	Communications
Lead production teams	Perform cost and price comparative analysis	Reports and Information Management
Maintained repeat customer clients	Compile budget information	
Menu planning	Recommend and implement changes	
New catering sales	Develop pricing and cost accounting procedures	
Personal needs of first family	Develop pricing and marketing information	
Petty cash funds	Direct staff	
Promote safe food handling	Create project timeline	
Purchasing, quality, and cost recommendations	Manage operations	
Quality assurance	Oversee vendor contracts	
Supervised staff	Information management	
Updated computer technology	Customer service	
Vending operations	Communication	

Fill in the Outline

Now that you have your outline, fill it in with descriptions of each skill set. You can find resume description content in your current resume, the vacancy announcement, other similar vacancy announcements, or the Classification Standards from the Office of Personnel Management website at www.opm.gov.

Below is a portion of the work experience section based on the outline headings for John Wallstone. You will be able to see many of the keywords in his resume.

Serve as second in command of kitchen staff for First Family of Maryland.

OPERATIONS MANAGEMENT: Direct daily operations of full-service kitchen, planning, coordinating, and preparing formal and informal meals and events for up to 3,000 people, both planned in advance and last minute, with range of guests from international dignitaries to constituents.

PROJECT MANAGEMENT: Conduct needs assessment surveys and determine needs based on event specifications and labor demands. Plan event with consideration to protocol, preferences, caliber of event, attendees, and lead time. Create project timeline and assign, monitor, and adjust tasks according to staff strengths/weaknesses to fulfill deadline completion.

SUPERVISOR / TEAM LEAD: Direct kitchen and wait staff, promoting teamwork and communication. Provide continual training and coaching to improve employee performance, job knowledge, and career advancement; also, serve as point of contact for benefit information. Resolve employee issues and provide employee input and feedback to management. Train others in security and privacy protection.

CUSTOMER SERVICES: Serve as personal and administrative assistant to First Family. Anticipate and respond to needs, maintaining flexible and service-oriented attitude. Assist in managing schedule and making travel arrangements and appointment reservations, as needed. Protect privacy of First Family and work with Maryland State Police to ensure security precautions are followed at all times.

SUPPLY MANAGEMENT: Take inventory and plan orders to regulate flow of product and ensure stock levels meet event and daily needs. Research best products and vendors to comply with state purchasing regulations; establish delivery protocols and resolve delivery problems. Rotate stock, monitor usage and storage to ensure efficiency, sanitation, and security, and reduce waste. Negotiate, administer, and oversee vendor and service contracts. Maintain documentation, verify invoices, and assure prompt payment.

BUDGETING AND FUND MANAGEMENT: Develop pricing and cost accounting procedures. Analyze and forecast product and labor cost estimates. Apply due diligence to projects to ensure feasibility and cost effectiveness, as well as conduct after-action reviews. Compile budget information and apply generally accepted accounting procedures and state regulations to track expenditures, including petty cash. Perform cost and price and comparative analyses. Develop and implement pricing and marketing information for clients. Identify and resolve budget issues and develop cost-cutting solutions to ensure budget adherence. Brief management and recommend cost control improvements and budget adjustments.

LOGISTICS MANAGEMENT: Integrate logistics of event planning, including manpower and personnel, supply, training, storage, and facilities. Research and plan manpower, equipment, and fiscal resources.

COMMUNICATIONS: Build rapport with internal staff and external departments to improve operations and flow of information. Respond to written and verbal inquires from the public and the media, adhering to strict communication standards. Represent First Family at charity and press events.

REPORTS AND INFORMATION MANAGEMENT: Develop and utilize spreadsheets, databases, and professional documents to improve operational readiness, manage projects, and research information. Maintain records on events, including menus, demographics, and after-action reports. Assist in establishing database for mailing list.

Remember Your Accomplishments

As a final step, John listed his main accomplishments. We will discuss how to write accomplishments for your resume in Step 7. Add the accomplishments into each skills bucket to link your accomplishments to specific skills. See the Outline Format USAJOBS federal resume starting on page 96 to see how the accomplishments are blended into the Outline Format.

- Plan, coordinate, and execute breakfast, lunch, and dinner for First Family and other events, including seated dinners and open houses for up to 4,000, with usually 3-5 events per week, as many as 2 per day.

- Instituted process changes to increase efficiency and change mind-set from reactive to proactive. Created plan to work one meal ahead, allowing time to respond to last minute requests, changes, and events.

- Received letter of appreciation from the White House for organizing luncheon attended by President Bill Clinton with less than 24-hour notice.

- Implemented industrial production system, automated systems, and information management for production, scheduling, and cost control.

- Managed a 425-person party, while in the process of hiring a new manager, short-staffed, family emergency for another chef, and just 10 days after 9/11 terrorists attacks. With lead time of 10 days, I used object-oriented planning, working backwards from the final outcome to the initial step. RESULTS: The event was a success; the guests and the client were very pleased. I demonstrated my skills as a planner, organizer, decision maker and crisis manager, solidifying my management's confidence in me as a project manager.

Important Federal Resume Writing Facts

Now that you have written the most difficult portion of your federal resume, it is time to put it all together and add the surrounding sections to make your resume complete. First, let us start with some important resume writing facts and tips.

- ✪ Federal resumes must include compliance details for each job for the last ten years. Compliance details include supervisor's name and telephone number; street address, including ZIP code; hours per week; and ending salary.

- ✪ Reverse chronology: Begin with your most recent position and work backward, unless you need to highlight a position that is relevant and not the most recent.

- ✪ Last ten years: Develop an outline, with compliance details, of all job-related positions help within the last ten years.

- ✪ Prior to ten years: If the positions are relevant, include the title of your job, organization, city, state, and dates. A short one-sentence description can be included. Prior to ten years, your supervisor's name, telephone number, specific address, zip codes, and salaries may not be relevant, correct, or needed any longer.

- ✪ Students: Include relevant positions only.

- ✪ Retired Military: Combine early positions/assignments.

- ✪ Unpaid volunteer experience is equal to paid work experience for federal job qualifications. You can write about volunteer and community service activities as though it is a job if it will help you qualify for a position. If you are using unpaid work to qualify, always include the number of hours per week in your description. If you have paid employment that qualifies you for the job, then simply summarize your volunteer experience under Community Service in the Additional Information section.

- ✪ Missing years of experience? Just skip those years and write great descriptions about the positions you have held. You do not need to describe reasons for a gap in your dates. However, be prepared to discuss it in an interview. Many people miss years of employment due to education, travel, and family responsibilities. The new federal resume focuses on experience that is relevant, and not on every job you held or every period in your life.

- ✪ Returning to government after leaving? Feature your government experience first, then list your business experience or other experience second. Even if it is out of the reverse chronology, the personnel specialists will want to see your government positions first.

- ✪ Any military assignments? List the most recent ones first. Include many details on the last ten years. Anything beyond than ten years, summarize and edit the text to include only the relevant experience.

Resume Writing Tips

✪ Use plain language. Write professionally and concisely.

✪ Eliminate acronyms whenever possible. When you must use them, spell them out the first time and separate with parentheses, commas, or dashes.

✪ Space is limited, so drop words that do not add value such as "responsible for," "very" and "duties include." Also, see how many times you can delete "the" without changing the meaning.

✪ Avoid using the same descriptor twice in the same paragraph, such as "manage," "develop," or "coordinate." Use a thesaurus to maximize descriptors and minimize repeating words.

✪ Start each sentence with an action verb, and not "I." Use the personal pronoun "I" two times per page, to remind the reader that it is YOUR resume.

✪ Active voice is more powerful than passive voice.

✪ Use present tense for present work experience, past tense for previous work experience or for projects in the present work experience that have ended. Do not add "s" to your verbs, i.e., "plans" or "leads," as this is writing in the third person. Write in the first person, without the use of "I."

✪ Use ALL CAPS for official position titles. This also holds true for titles of roles in jobs, or unofficial, working job titles, such as PROJECT MANAGER, SENIOR STAFF ADVISOR, RECEPTIONIST, when you are describing these in your work experience summary.

✪ All caps can be used to identify major functional areas of work. Keep your paragraph length to eight to ten lines.

✪ Use more nouns. Nouns are searchable terms in most databases. If you can use "editor" rather than "responsible for compiling documents and preparing a publication," you will be more successful.

✪ Include the proper names and generic descriptions of products, software, and equipment. It is difficult to know which words will be in a database. Write both to be sure.

✪ KSAs in the resume? You will read some vacancy announcements that say you should include the Knowledge, Skills, and Abilities in the resume. Use the outline format to cover your KSAs, using the keywords from the KSAs in the outline headlines to bring attention to your KSAs.

✪ You do not have to rewrite the entire resume for every vacancy announcement, but it is helpful if you identify the top five to seven skills and change the ALL CAP headings to match each announcement. You could also move the paragraphs around to emphasize the most important skills for each position.

✪ Do not upload your resume as a document in the USAJOBS resume system. Use the resume builder to copy and paste your resume content into USAJOBS, so that the resume will include all of the information required. You can then preview your resume to see the final result.

Steps to Creating Your USAJOBS Federal Resume

Your resume is EVERYTHING—your entire application. So, take your time and add all of the information you can to demonstrate your specialized experience for the federal position.

To get started, we recommend that you first create a "basic resume." Create this first version (according to the instructions in this book) in your word processing file and save it on your computer. Do not write the resume inside the USAJOBS resume builder.

Complete these resume sections in the following order:

1. Candidate Information
2. Work Experience
   - Create your Outline Format with Headlines
   - Fill in your duties, responsibilities, and projects
   - Include recognitions
   - Add bullets to feature KSAs in the resume
3. Education and Training
4. Additional Information, including a Profile Statement

More information about each section is provided on the following pages.

Count characters while you are writing your Work Experience sections. You are allowed 3,000 characters, including spaces, in each Work Experience job block. If you need more space, you can continue in the Additional Information section.

When you add bullets, the bullets can be copied and pasted into USAJOBS. The resume sample in this chapter demonstrates bullet formatting in the USAJOBS builder.

After you have completed your first draft, copy and paste the resume content from your word processing file into the USAJOBS Resume builder. It will take you about one hour to copy and paste your resume content into the USAJOBS builder.

If you are applying for different types of positions, it is a good idea to repeat the steps above to create a basic resume for each type of position. Be sure to give your resumes names of the positions you are seeking, i.e., Program Analyst, GS 11, FEMA; or Administrative Assistant, GS 7, SBA; or Budget Analyst, GS 14, OPM. This will help you remember how you focused each resume and will make your resume more search friendly.

As you apply for jobs, you must go back into your basic resume and add the keywords and skills for EACH announcement before you submit your resume. It is helpful to save a copy of every resume that you submit.

Once your USAJOBS resume is ready, Step 8 will help you understand how to apply for positions with your resume.

Universal Formatting Instructions for Different Resume Builders

✪ Write targeted versions of your resume for each application, picking up keywords and skills from the announcement.

✪ KSA accomplishments can stand out with bullets.

✪ Research and include key skills.

✪ Follow the character counts for each resume builder.

✪ Use ALL CAPS for highlighting job titles or other important nouns.

✪ Do not overuse all caps.

✪ Do not use bold, italics, underlining, or other special fonts.

✪ Do not use lines, borders, or boxes.

✪ Do not use a two-column format.

✪ Keep paragraphs to eight to ten lines maximum.

✪ Add a hard return between paragraphs to improve readability and add white space.

✪ Most resume builders give you space for six jobs.

✪ Copy and paste your resume into the resume builders.

✪ Keep your passwords.

Helpful Tools for Writing Your Federal Resume

The Resume Place has a free Federal Resume Builder at www.resume-place.com. You can also access our Federal Resume Database with over 400 resume samples to jump start your own resume at www.resume-place.com/books/books-online-federal-resume-database/.

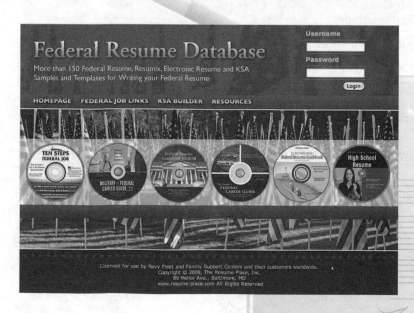

The USAJOBS Resume Builder Section by Section

Confidentiality

Indicate whether you want your personal information to remain confidential for resume searches. If your resume is public (searchable), employers (not other USAJOB members) can find your resume during resume searches. Because employers may search for candidates before they post a job on USAJOBS, choosing the public option will give you the widest possible access to job opportunities. In this section of the resume builder, you have the option keep your resume public but hide your contact info, current company, and references. Employers will be able to contact you through your confidential USAJOBS email address, and you can view the job listing and decide whether to respond. The confidentiality preference ONLY applies to resume searches; if you apply online with your posted resume, ALL information, including the information you marked as confidential, will be shown to the employer.

Candidate Information

Much of your compliance information is included in the USAJOBS profile set-up. Here are the typical personal compliance details that civil service human resources offices require:

- ✪ Full name, mailing address (with zip code), email address, and day and evening phone numbers (with area code)
- ✪ Social security number
- ✪ Country of citizenship
- ✪ Veterans' preference
- ✪ Selective Service registration status

For your online security, the following personal information should never be included:

- ✪ National identification number
- ✪ Driver's license number
- ✪ Bank account information
- ✪ Credit card information
- ✪ Passwords
- ✪ Date of birth

Highest Career Level Achieved

This information is optional and not necessary for current or former federal employees.

Federal Employee Information

Fill in "no," unless you are or were a federal civilian employee who holds or held a non-temporary appointment.

Work Experience

We have discussed this section at length earlier in this step. Copy and paste your work into the Work Experience section.

Include Recognitions in Job Descriptions

Most federal announcements give instructions that you cannot attach letters of commendation to the application. Therefore, the best way to include a quote from an evaluation or letter is to include a quote from the commendation in the Work Experience section of your resume. Collect any emails or complimentary letters you have received from supervisors, customers, or other important individuals that say you are an outstanding employee or supervisor.

The following letters are possible sources to review for good quotes:

- ✪ Outstanding team reviews (as a member or leader of a team)
- ✪ Outstanding performance ratings
- ✪ Customer satisfaction awards or letters
- ✪ Write-ups in company newsletters
- ✪ Employee of the month recognitions
- ✪ Community or volunteer service recognitions
- ✪ Newspaper quotes

Honors from outside organizations, recognition for community service, or achievements from your academic or civic background can also reinforce recognition of your skills.

Quote Recognitions and Awards

The following are a few examples of how to use the quoted material in your resume:

- ✪ Received Letter of Commendation from the Chief of Naval Material, 20xx.
- ✪ For planning, acquiring, and implementing a CAD/CAM system at 54 Navy sites, received a "Special Act Award" for my accomplishments under this project.

Education

List your educational credentials, such as: high school diploma, FED, certifications, vocational training, college coursework completed, associate degree, bachelor's degree, master's degree, doctorate, or professional degree. If you are currently earning a degree, you can indicate the expected date of completion. Be aware that the instructions say to "only list degrees from schools that have been accredited by accrediting institutions recognized by the U.S. Department of Education or education that meet the provisions in the Office of Personnel Management's Operating Manual."

Sample

EDUCATION

B.S., Management & Marketing / Finance Minor, 12/19xx, Texas Tech University
GPA: 2.9 out of 4.0; 120 +Semester Hours

RELEVANT COURSEWORK: Economics, Accounting, Cost Accounting, Business Policy & Development, Marketing, Finance, Business Finance, Business Law, International Business.

COMPUTER/TECHNICAL SKILLS: DMSi, Microsoft Office (Word, Excel, PowerPoint, Access). Working knowledge of Access, Lotus, WordPerfect.

Job Related Training

For the last five to ten years, list the title of each relevant course and year completed. Include recent computer and technical courses.

Sample 1

Continuing Education and Training

[date] How to Prepare a Quality IT Offer 0.1 Credits

[date] GSA Vendor Payment Update 0.1 Credits

[date] AM e-Authentication 0.1 Credits

[date] Secure Wireless Technology 0.1 Credits

[date] Proper Use of Non-DoD Contracts 1.0 Credit

[date] GWAC Direct Order Direct Bill Authority 0.1 Credits

[date] Marketing Strategies and Techniques for Small Business 0.1 Credits

[date] The 1102 Contract Specialist as a Business Manager 0.1 Credits

---

Sample 2

SALES AND MARKETING PROFESSIONAL DEVELOPMENT COURSES

Law of Agency, Real Estate College, Arlington, TX, 30 credit hours, [mo/year]

MS Software Application Training, Work In Texas, Dallas, TX, 10 credit hours, [mo/year]

Acquisition/Procurement Planning I Certification, Management Concepts, Washington, DC, 80 credit hours, [mo/year]

References / Additional Language Skills / Affiliations / Professional Publications

These sections are self-explanatory, but you have questions, click on the blue question mark button for guidance.

Additional Information / Other Qualifications and Skills

The "Additional Information" field in USAJOBS is a great place to list your summary of skills, areas of expertise, and positions that were part-time or volunteer. You can also list travel experiences and special interests. Include a profile statement (more information on the next page).

Additional Information Ideas:

- Associations
- Community Service
- Computer Skills
- Conferences Attended
- Consultancies

- Honors & Awards
- International Travel
- Memberships/Office Activities
- Part-Time Jobs

- Presentations
- Publications
- Special Interests
- Teaching Positions
- Volunteer Services

Samples

PROFESSIONAL DEGREES, DESIGNATIONS & LICENSES

- Real Estate Broker
- B100 Unlimited General Contractor's license state of Utah
- Certified Insurance Consultant
- Investment Advisor under the 1940 Act
- NASD Principal's License, DPP/BD, Series 6, 22, 39, 63

PERSONAL ACCOMPLISHMENTS

- Private Pilot – Instrument rated
- Commercial Pilot – Hot Air Balloons
- Climbed Kilimanjaro, Huascuran, Rainier
- Only American crewmember on the Soviet team for the Whitbread Round the World race, Ft. Lauderdale to Southampton, England leg, aboard "Fazisi"
- Vice President, Kyrgyz National Biathlon Federation

AVOCATIONS

- Woodworking, Rowing, Skiing, Reading

Availability, Specific Work Environment, Desired Locations

Select all that you can possibly accept, especially Temp and Term positions, which could turn into a full-time position in the future. Regarding location, do not assume that you will receive relocation expenses.

Writing a Profile Statement

You will want to summarize your entire career into one amazing paragraph—your profile statement—in case the HR specialist or manager would like to read a short summary of your experience. Feature the most impressive skills and expertise in your profile statement.

Very often in job interviews, an employer will open by saying, "Tell me about yourself." The "Profile" paragraph provides an opportunity to develop a precise and targeted response with the keywords and skills from the Duties section of the announcement. For career change resumes, the profile or summary of skills is critical for featuring the skills and most relevant experience for the next career.

The following examples show two formats for profile statements.

Sample 1

- BUSINESS DEVELOPMENT: Experienced business developer with outstanding strategic, technical, and organizational leadership skills. Comfortable advising others who are interested in tackling new business start-up challenges. Known for the ability to collaborate with individuals and teams to develop business strategies and manage specific components of strategies to meet measurable performance benchmarks. Recognized as an expert in private sector development, including host-country economic development programs and policies, having served as a Country Director (GS-15) in the Peace Corps, in Kyrgyzstan.

- BUSINESS ACUMEN: Excellent business instincts, including financial and human resource allocation, and leveraging technological resources. Demonstrated ability to provide exceptional customer services by assessing customer needs, meeting quality standards, and evaluating customer satisfaction.

- LEADER OF CHANGE: Accomplished at leading change, starting new companies, and taking them from conceptualization through to completion, also reorganizing existing companies. Skilled at evaluating, negotiating, planning, budgeting, and administering projects and proposals with an emphasis on dollar productive activities. Ability to convince others of the value of a specific course of action.

- GOVERNMENT ISSUES: Intensely curious about how things work in politics, the world of investing, community affairs, business, and governmental issues. Always willing to seek the advice of experts in various fields before coming to a conclusion or final decision.

Sample 2

Information Technology Director with an outstanding record of success delivering enterprise applications and architectures for federal and commercial organizations. Extensive experience developing short and long term Information Technology (IT) strategies, practices, policies, and metrics for highly technical and agile organizations in the public and private sectors. Experienced in all phases of the Software Development Life Cycle (SDLC) from requirements analysis through user acceptance and operational support. Combine results-oriented project management skills with expert technical knowledge of network and IT service offerings to deliver best value solutions for the customer. A decisive and participatory leader with keen business acumen, motivating leadership skills, and extensive knowledge of emerging trends in the information age.

Highlighting One Year Specialized Experience

Once you have a draft of your Outline Format resume, go back to your target vacancy announcement and read the Qualifications section again. Look at the One Year Specialized Experience instruction and review the keywords. Make sure that your resume hits this specialized experience with examples. We have talked about keywords in this book many times.

When reviewing applications, the HR specialist will be looking for the relevant experience for their position. So, in your work experience, the positions that are most relevant to your target position should be the most in-depth and carefully written. Outstanding resumes keep the reader's attention longer, compelling the reader to move the resume to the "read again later" pile, then with further reading, to the "Best Qualified" list. The selecting official will go through the same process.

Final Tips

Highlight your skills!

> The goal of the organization and presentation in your resume is to highlight the skills that support your federal job objective. Make sure that the keywords are in the resume in either the HEADLINES or the text. You want to make it easy for the human resources staff to find the information needed to ensure you are qualified for the job.

Modify your basic resume for various builders and announcements

Your basic resume can be used for various resume builders, but you will need to change your resume each time you apply for a new job, because the keywords are different for every vacancy announcement. When switching between builders, make sure to count characters and follow the instructions carefully.

Review the critical job elements

Review the duties in the vacancy announcement against your resume AGAIN. Make sure the keywords in the Duties section are visible, that the One Year Specialized Experience is clearly presented, that examples they are seeking are included, and that you have utilized the space in the builder correctly.

Read your resume aloud and edit profusely!

Now that you have drafted your basic federal resume, you will need to edit and decide what is relevant and most important for the position. Most public service resumes are two to five pages in length. However, length is not the most important element of the resume—content is.

Sample USAJOBS Federal Resume Work Experience Section in Outline Format with KSAs in the Resume

	John Wallstone 123 Dewberry Way Baltimore, MD 21243 Day Phone: 410 123-4567 Email: jwallstonecraft@gmail.com
WORK EXPERIENCE	Government House, State of Maryland 4/2003 – Present Annapolis, MD US Salary: $60,000 USD Per Year Hours per week: 70 SOUS CHEF Serve as second in command of kitchen staff for First Family of Maryland.
ALL CAPS outline headings	OPERATIONS MANAGEMENT: Direct daily operations of full-service kitchen, planning, coordinating, and preparing formal and informal meals and events for up to 3,000 people, both planned in advance and last minute, with range of guests from international dignitaries to constituents.
Key accomplish-ments are bullets under each outline heading	• Plan, coordinate, and execute breakfast, lunch, and dinner for First Family and other events, including seated dinners and open houses for up to 4,000, with usually 3-5 events per week, as many as 2 per day. • Implemented industrial production system, automated systems and information management for production, scheduling, and cost control.
ALL CAPS outline headings	PROJECT MANAGEMENT: Conduct needs assessment surveys and determine needs based on event specifications and labor demands. Plan event with consideration to protocol, preferences, caliber of event, attendees, and lead time. Create project timeline and assign, monitor, and adjust tasks according to staff strengths/weaknesses to fulfill deadline completion.
Key accomplish-ments are bullets under each outline heading	• Received letter of appreciation from the White House for organizing luncheon attended by President Bill Clinton with less than 24-hour notice. • Instituted process changes to increase efficiency and change mind-set from reactive to proactive. Created plan to work one meal ahead, allowing time to respond to last minute requests, changes, and events. • Managed a 425-person party, while in the process of hiring a new manager, short-staffed, family emergency for another chef, and just 10 days after 9/11 terrorists attacks. With lead time of 10 days, I used object-oriented planning, working backwards from the final outcome to the initial step. RESULTS: The event was a success; the guests and the client were very pleased. I demonstrated my skills as a planner, organizer, decision maker and crisis manager, solidifying my management's confidence in me as a project manager.

WORK EXPERIENCE continued	SUPERVISOR / TEAM LEAD: Direct kitchen and wait staff, promoting teamwork and communication. Provide continual training and coaching to improve employee performance, job knowledge, and career advancement; also, serve as point of contact for benefit information. Resolve employee issues and provide employee input and feedback to management. Train others in security and privacy protection.

• When I first started at Government House, communications between State Troopers (security) departments and in the kitchen were abysmal. I made a direct effort to change the environment, using my interpersonal skills to make the office more open and cooperative. If I learned information the troopers could use, I shared it with them. Information has included number of parties held and client demographics. RESULTS: Since instituting my team-first approach and actively building relationships, the atmosphere at Government House was improved on many levels. The final result was better service to the First Family and more efficient operations. CONTINUED IN ADDITIONAL INFORMATION

Quality Food Service Corporation
12/2000 - 2/2003
Silver Spring, MD US
Salary: $38,000 USD Per Year
Hours per week: 40

FOOD AND BEVERAGE DIRECTOR; EXECUTIVE CHEF

Held two positions with this international food and facilities management company. Hired as Executive Chef for Spirit of Washington; promoted to Food and Beverage Director in May 19xx.

FOOD AND BEVERAGE DIRECTOR: Executive Dining Room: BellSouth Network Services. Designed and directed production of breakfast and lunch menus for service 5 days a week, for 100 employees. Supervised staff of 8. Served as point of contact for BellSouth management. Updated computer technology to modernize purchasing and just in time inventory systems. Developed marketing and advertising campaigns to increase business. Installed accounting and customer service tracking systems. Introduced and maintained hazardous area critical control points program to promote safe food handling. Managed a 70-machine vending operation.

• Increased new catering sales and established new client services. Developed and led employee customer service and food production and sanitation training sessions.

EXECUTIVE CHEF: Spirit of Washington: Led galley team of 20 employees and two supervisors. Employed commercial and banquet-style food production methods to achieve time and product management. Directed purchasing, inventory control, and training involved with menu execution. Achieved increased efficiencies in purchasing, inventory, and scheduling using computer technology. Developed and trained employees in new sanitation and food safety training programs. Recognized by management for improvements to product quality, cost effectiveness, and employee morale.

• Oversaw menu design, coordination, and execution for lunch, dinner, and catered events on 450-passenger vessel.

EDUCATION	Undergraduate Coursework, Computer Programming, Anne Arundel Community College, Arnold, MD, 2002-2003, 12 credits
	A.A., Restaurant Cooking Skills, Baltimore International College, Baltimore, MD, 1991
	B.S., Business Administration, Shepherd University, Shepherdstown, WV, 1990
	Diploma, Easton Senior High, Easton, MD, 1984
TRAINING	Workplace Sexual Harassment Training, 9/2001
	Workplace Diversity Training, 4 hours, 7/2001
	Front Line Leadership, 12 hours, 6/1995
ADDITIONAL INFORMATION	SOUS CHEF, STATE OF MARYLAND GOVERNOR'S MANSION CONTINUED
	CUSTOMER SERVICES: Serve as personal and administrative assistant to First Family. Anticipate and respond to needs, maintaining flexible and service-oriented attitude. Assist in managing schedule and making travel arrangements and appointment reservations, as needed. Protect privacy of First Family and work with Maryland State Police to ensure security precautions are followed at all times.
	SUPPLY MANAGEMENT: Take inventory and plan orders to regulate flow of product and ensure stock levels meet event and daily needs. Research best products and vendors to comply with state purchasing regulations; establish delivery protocols and resolve delivery problems. Rotate stock, monitor usage and storage to ensure efficiency, sanitation, and security, and reduce waste. Negotiate, administer, and oversee vendor and service contracts. Maintain documentation, verify invoices, and assure prompt payment.
	BUDGETING AND FUND MANAGEMENT: Develop pricing and cost accounting procedures. Analyze and forecast product and labor costs estimates. Apply due diligence to projects to ensure feasibility and cost effectiveness, as well as conduct after-action reviews. Compile budget information and apply generally accepted accounting procedures and state regulations to track expenditures, including petty cash. Perform cost and price and comparative analyses. Develop and implement pricing and marketing information for clients. Identify and resolve budget issues and develop cost-cutting solutions to ensure budget adherence. Brief management and recommend cost control improvements and budget adjustments.
	LOGISTICS MANAGEMENT: Integrate logistics of event planning, including manpower and personnel, supply, training, storage, and facilities. Research and plan manpower, equipment, and fiscal resources.

ADDITIONAL INFORMATION	COMMUNICATIONS: Build rapport with internal staff and external departments to improve operations and flow of information. Respond to written and verbal inquires from the public and the media, adhering to strict communication standards. Represent First Family at charity and press events.

• Actively built team mind-set and morale and implemented employee incentive program, stressing interdepartmental cooperation and employees' role in organizational success. Resulted in improved attendance and performance.

REPORTS AND INFORMATION MANAGEMENT: Develop and utilize spreadsheets, databases, and professional documents to improve operational readiness, manage projects, and research information. Maintain records on events, including menus, demographics, and after-action reports. Assist in establishing database for mailing list.

AWARDS / HONORS

Received outstanding evaluations and awarded highest incentive 5 years in a row under the State of Maryland Pay for Performance Program

Received Governor's Citation for participation and assistance in Wye River Peace Talks, 1998

COMPUTER PROFICIENCIES

MS Office: Word, Excel, Outlook, PowerPoint, Access; C Language Programming, Adobe Acrobat

VOLUNTEER EXPERIENCE

Participated in the Meals on Wheels Chefs Expo Fundraiser, 2005

Represented Government House in a television spot for Baltimore WJZ 11, 2004

Attended educational speaking engagements on Career Days at Westview Elementary and Anne Arundel County High schools, 2002-2003

PROFESSIONAL PROFILE:

Over 12 years of management experience in state government and corporate settings. Demonstrated expertise in project management, team building, analysis, budget management, and improving operations. Able to assess needs, processes, and performance and recommend and implement improvements. Strong skills in customer service, as well as interpersonal, written and verbal communications. Excellent ability to establish priorities, multi-task, and meet strict deadlines. Proven proficiency in developing innovative solutions to problems and achieving results.

The only time you might still need a paper version of your federal resume is for networking purposes. John Wallstone's short one- to two-page networking resume is shown here.

JOHN WALLSTONE

123 Dewberry Way • Baltimore, MD 21243
Residence: 410-123-4567 • Office: 202-123-4567
Email: jwallstonecraft@gmail.com

Citizenship: U.S.

Veteran's Preference: N/A
Candidate Source: External

PROFILE: Over 12 years of management experience in government and corporate settings. Demonstrated expertise in budget management, project management, team building and improving operations. Able to assess needs, processes and performance and recommend and implement improvements. Strong skills in customer service, as well as interpersonal, written and verbal communications. Excellent ability to establish priorities, multi-task and meet strict deadlines. Proven proficiency in developing innovative solutions to problems and achieving results.

PROFESSIONAL EMPLOYMENT

Sous Chef, Government House, State of Maryland

Annapolis, MD   04/2003 - Present

Serve as second in command of kitchen staff for First Family of Maryland. Manage kitchen operations and direct staff to ensure efficient business processes and customer satisfaction.

Operations Management: Direct daily operations of full-service kitchen, planning, coordinating, and preparing formal and informal meals and events for up to 3,000 people, both planned in advance and last minute, with range of guests from international dignitaries to constituents.

Project Management, Analysis and Workflow Management: Conduct needs assessment surveys and determine needs based on event specifications and labor demands. Plan event with consideration to protocol, preferences, caliber of event, attendees, and lead time.

Key Accomplishments:

- Plan, coordinate, and execute breakfast, lunch, dinner for First Family and other events, including seated dinners and open houses for up to 4,000, with usually 3-5 events per week, as many as 2 per day.

- Instituted process changes to increase efficiency and change mind-set from reactive to proactive. Created plan to work one meal ahead, allowing time to respond to last minute requests, changes, and events.

- Received letter of appreciation from the White House for organizing luncheon attended by President Bill Clinton with less than 24-hour notice.

- Implemented industrial production system, automated systems and information management for production, scheduling, and cost control.

- Actively built team mind-set and morale and implemented employee incentive program, stressing interdepartmental cooperation and employees' role in organizational success. Resulted in improved attendance and performance.

Supply Management: Take inventory and plan orders to regulate flow of product and ensure stock levels meet event and daily needs.

Budgeting / Funds Management: Develop pricing and cost accounting procedures. Analyze and forecast product and labor cost estimates.

Personnel Management: Direct kitchen and wait staff, promoting teamwork and communication. Provide continual training and coaching to improve employee performance, job knowledge, and career advancement.

Customer Service: Serve as personal and administrative assistant to First Family. Anticipate and respond to needs, maintaining flexible and service-oriented attitude.

Information Management: Develop and utilize spreadsheets, databases, and professional documents to improve operational readiness, manage projects, and research information.

Food and Beverage Director; Executive Chef, Qualify Food Service Corporation
Silver Spring, MD   12/2000 - 02/2003

Food and Beverage Director, Executive Dining Room: BellSouth Network Services. Designed and directed production of breakfast and lunch menus for service 5 days a week, for 100 employees. Supervised staff of 8. Served as point of contact for BellSouth management. Increased new catering sales and established new client services.

Executive Chef, Spirit of Washington: Oversaw menu design, coordination, and execution for lunch, dinner, and catered events on 450-passenger vessel. Lcd galley team of 20 employees and two supervisors.

EDUCATION
- A.A., Restaurant Cooking Skills, Baltimore International College, Baltimore, MD, 1991
- B.S., Business Administration, Shepherd University, Shepherdstown, WV, 1990

TRAINING
- Workplace Sexual Harassment Training, 9/2001
- Workplace Diversity Training, 4 hours, 7/2001
- Front Line Leadership, 12 hours, 6/1995

AWARDS / HONORS
- Received outstanding evaluations and awarded highest incentive 5 years in a row under the State of Maryland Pay for Performance Program
- Received Governor's Citation for participation and assistance in Wye River Peace Talks, 1998

COMPUTER PROFICIENCIES: MS Office: Word, Excel, Outlook, PowerPoint, Access;
C Language Programming, Adobe Acrobat

VOLUNTEER EXPERIENCE
- Participated in the Meals on Wheels Chefs Expo Fundraiser, 2005
- Represented Government House in a television spot for Baltimore WJZ 11, 2004
- Attended educational speaking engagements on Career Days at Westview Elementary and Anne Arundel County High schools, 2002-2003

STEP SEVEN

Conquer the KSAs in the Resume and the Questionnaires

Haven't KSAs Been Eliminated?

Even though the separate narrative KSAs have mostly been eliminated from the USAJOBS announcements by the November 2010 Hiring Reform, the KSAs still live on in different forms:

✪ as KSAs that should be included in your resume,

✪ in the questionnaires, and

✪ as questions in the Behavior-Based Interview.

Therefore, this step still covers the methods of writing KSAs. You will still need to prepare the KSAs in order to become Best Qualified for the position you are seeking, but now you will be adapting them to different lengths for each of the purposes above. We recommend about 300 to 400 characters for KSA accomplishments in the resume and a longer version for behavior-based interviews.

Top Tips for Writing Winning KSA Narratives

#1 Give one fantastic example per KSA. KSAs are no place to talk in generalities. Get very specific about what you did and your results.

#2 Quantify or qualify your results/accomplishments. It is better to say that you type 65 wpm than to say you type fast. It is better to say that you came in $12,000 below budget than to say you saved your office money.

#3 Let the CCAR drive your story. Context-Challenge-Actions-Results is a winning formula.

#4 Try www.resume-place.com/ksabuilder for writing your CCAR KSAs! (screenshot on right)

KSA BUILDER AND THE CCAR

The KSA Builder follows the Context-Challenge-Action-Results model for writing examples that will demonstrate your Knowledge, Skills and Abilities. This format gives the staffing specialist and hiring manager readable, interesting and specific examples that they can rate and rank based on the hiring manager's requirements.

Each KSA Builder Form contains fields for writing two examples that support each KSA.

Results: What happened? (quantify with numbers if possible)

Example 2.
Please fill in the following fields to give the human resources staff (another example) of your experience which supports this particular KSA.

Context: Your title and office and dates

Challenge: What was the challenge?

Action: What action did you take?
1.

What is a KSA or Questionnaire?

Even though the KSA narratives were eliminated as part of the application, the KSAs or competencies needed for a particular position still appear in most USAJOBS vacancy announcements to be covered in your resume as mini-KSAs or short accomplishments.

The purpose of the KSAs and questionnaires is to help the hiring officials screen out applicants who do not have the specialized experience needed for the job and to help identify the best qualified applicant. Think of KSAs as basically pre-interview questions. The questionnaire serves the same purpose but is most often a set of multiple choice questions addressing the skills that you will use on the job. If you do have the skills and abilities to perform the job, this part of your application will give you the opportunity to express your strengths more thoroughly.

Another important point is this: the KSAs and questionnaires are scored like an examination. So, you need to pay attention to the questions in the KSAs and questionnaires just like you are taking an exam for the position.

It can be confusing at times to delineate clearly what is a skill, what is an ability, and what is knowledge. Here is how the government defines each of these terms:

⊛ Knowledge: An organized body of information, usually of a factual or procedural nature, which, if applied, makes adequate performance on the job possible.

⊛ Skills: The proficient manual, verbal, or mental manipulation of data, people, or things. Observable, quantifiable, and measurable.

⊛ Abilities: The power to perform an activity at the present time. Implied is a lack of discernible barriers, either physical or mental, to performing the activity.

Agencies do not always call KSA statements "Knowledge, Skills, and Abilities." They might also be called competencies or selective placement factors.

Commonly Seen KSAs

For many positions, especially in general administrative and management positions, you will likely encounter KSAs that ask you to address seemingly basic knowledge, skills, and abilities in your resume. These are some of the commonly seen factors:

⊛ Communicate orally and/or in writing
⊛ Plan and organize work (for yourself or for others)
⊛ Independently plan and carry out multiple assignments
⊛ Locate and assemble information for various reports, briefings, and conferences
⊛ Analyze and solve problems
⊛ Work well with others

Your KSA accomplishments will be scored based on your experiences. For example, you may earn five points for your ability to use Excel to create complex spreadsheets that contain formulas versus two points for the ability to enter data into Excel spreadsheets. For best success, explain the most complex level of performance you have ascertained in your experience that demonstrates your competence, and tell that story using keywords and phrases from the vacancy announcement.

Troutman Method Lesson 5:
Write KSAs Using the Context-Challenge-Action-Results Formula

Whether your KSAs are for your resume, questionnaires, or the interview, they should be focused around your accomplishments. Ideally, you have already completed Step 3 and have several excellent examples from which to choose.

When writing your KSAs, think of it as telling your story about your accomplishment. To see the whole story, your reader needs to know what you did, why you did it, how you did it, and what you accomplished. This is what is known as the CCAR approach, which stands for CONTEXT, CHALLENGE, ACTION, and RESULTS. The CCAR method is tried and true for developing any type of narrative to highlight your accomplishment, whether for job applications, job interviews, or self-assessments.

Let's define these terms specifically:

- ✪ Context: (Why you did it) Explain the factors contributing to the challenge you faced and the surrounding environment and circumstances. What job title did you hold and what was your level of responsibility? Why did you do what you did in the first place? Budget limits? Staffing changes? Institutional reform? New goals handed down from on high?

- ✪ Challenge: (Problems you faced) State the specific problem you had to address. For example, if the context included widespread institutional reform, what was the specific challenge you faced in your corner of the world that was caused by it and how did you respond to that reform?

- ✪ Action: (What you did and how you did it) Describe the specific steps you took to solve the problem, meet the goal, etc. Generally, it is best NOT to use ordinary examples. Just doing your basic job is not all that remarkable. Instead, look for instances where you took action that went above and beyond the call of duty, applied particularly creative ideas, or put forth Herculean effort. Seek the extraordinary action in what you did.

- ✪ Results: (What you accomplished) Show the outcome of your actions and the difference you made. Quantify your results whenever you can possibly do so. For example, "My quick thinking saved our department $17,000." Again, ignore any examples with mediocre results. Write only about the best you have done.

The CCAR is the crux of your story. It is the core of the KSA that demonstrates your Knowledge, Skills, or Abilities. However, a successful KSA will also feature a strong opening paragraph and an ending with impact. These paragraphs also give you an opportunity to give impressive information beyond your one strong accomplishment. In this way you can show that you understand the agency's mission or tell how many years you have been working in the field.

Turning an Accomplishment into a CCAR Narrative

In this example, you can see how one item from an accomplishment list can become a CCAR story that demonstrates your knowledge, skills, or abilities in a particular area.

CASE NAME: Jane Addams

PRIOR POSITION: Acting Manager of Customer Support / Customer Support Specialist

TARGET FEDERAL JOB: Information Technology Specialist, GS-2210-12/13

KSA Factor: *Skill in applying analytical and evaluative techniques and methods to complex technical problems to identify, develop, and propose viable alternatives and long-term solutions.*

CONTEXT: During my 25-year career in information technology, I have relied on my skills in analyzing and evaluating technical problems, recommending and developing viable solutions. I have resolved issues in software development, configuration and installation, as well as business process and operations problems.

CHALLENGE: In my first assignment at USPTO, I led a software development effort to improve process monitoring during peak times and load balancing for the group that monitored text search jobs on the Amdahl mainframe computer system. Specifically, I was challenged with delivering a solution that was user-friendly, easy to maintain, and could be delivered in a short timeframe.

ACTIONS: With my team of two developers, I met with the text search (Messenger) support group to determine business requirements. Identifying that simplicity of operations was the key to success, I proposed the system be written in REXX, as opposed to PL/1. This would allow changes to be made quickly and not require that the code be compiled; rather, it would just be moved from the Configuration Management (CM) area to the production area. This step would prevent mistakes and possible human error. I also proposed that the data tables for the program be external to the code and not under CM control. Instead, the master tables would be placed in CM and, unless corrupt, the Messenger group could change parameters to adjust load balancing daily.

My team designed and coded an interactive system to their requirements. We received approval from USPTO for the data tables to be external and began the testing phase. During testing, we discovered that starting additional processes this way required that the job be entered into a "super user" group. I assessed the impact and determined alternatives, briefing USPTO on the issue and options, and ultimately receiving a waiver to allow the project to continue.

RESULTS: My team delivered the completed project to the Messenger group on time and within budget. We also provided training and documentation beyond the original statement of work. This program ran successfully, without bug reports, for several years.

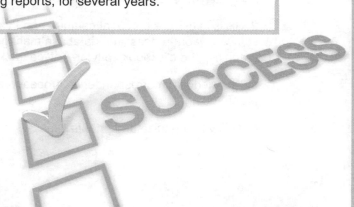

KSA Formats

Agencies consider a number of factors in determining the most appropriate assessment strategy for a particular position. Today's federal applications typically use one of these formats:

1. KSAs that are combined into the resume

2. Questionnaires with multiple choice questions

KSA narratives on a separate sheet are usually not required any longer, based on the President's Hiring Reform, but it is good to prepare the KSA narratives to get ready for your behavior-based interview. Try to prepare four to six KSAs for the interview (or for the application if you do get a rare instance of needing to submit separate KSAs).

KSAs in the Resume

Some KSAs are not statements, questions, or essays at all. They are merely knowledge, skills, and abilities that should be talked about in your resume using the federal resume outline format. In this case, the KSA factors provide you perfect insight into what the HR specialist will be looking for in the resume. It is your road map to success. You know exactly what your resume needs to say in order to rate well in the application. Because the announcement encourages you to "demonstrate" your experience, featuring accomplishments in the resume that show your competence in these areas is the best way to address them. Your description of your duties and responsibilities can also be used to cover these KSAs.

Sometimes KSAs that should be addressed in the resume are not labeled this clearly. In the absence of specific instructions, you may get in touch with the point of contact listed in the announcement to clarify.

Vacancy Announcement Example

HOW YOU WILL BE EVALUATED:

KSA(s) should be reflected within the experience history and not as a separate document. You will be evaluated to determine if you meet the minimum qualifications required; and on the extent to which your application shows that you possess the knowledge, skills and abilities associated with this position as defined below. When describing your knowledge, skills and abilities, please be sure to give examples and explain how often you used these skills, the complexity of the knowledge you possessed, the level of the people you interacted with, the sensitivity of the issues you handled, etc. Applicants are strongly encouraged to address how your experience demonstrates each of these factors to receive full consideration.

1. Knowledge of the military organization and agencies to effectively research and accurately refer customers to appropriate contacts.

2. Skills in using a personal computer and various computer applications; Microsoft Office software; work-processing, database management, desktop publishing, spreadsheets, graphics, and clickbook software, office tracker software.

3. Knowledge of correspondence procedures and skills in writing and editing and proofreading.

4. Ability to organize and prioritize tasks.

Questionnaires with Supporting Essays

As HR specialists seek more efficient ways to assess applicants, and as additional technology becomes readily available, the self-assessment questionnaire is becoming common in federal applications. In this format, you take an online examination to test your level of competence with the knowledge, skills, and abilities required for the position to be filled. Typically, you answer a series of multiple choice or yes/no answers where YOU indicate your level of performance and experience. The number of questions can range from two to more than 100! As with any part of the application, read them carefully to ensure you are answering accurately and following the instructions.

These questionnaires are popular with federal HR specialists, because the computer automatically grades the assessment, eliminating much of the work of reviewing hundreds of applications. Once the preliminary score is assigned, any corresponding essays, as well as the resume, are reviewed to determine your level of qualifications. To have success with this method of assessment, you must be able to select the highest-scoring answer for almost every question. The best strategy for mastering a self-assessment questionnaire is to consider how you can match an example from your list of accomplishments to the high-scoring answer. Again, only one accomplishment or example of performing that task is needed.

TIP: Your questionnaire answers MUST match the information in your resume. If you use the same resume for all of your applications, that one resume may not match the questionnaire. Compare your resume to the questions and update your resume to demonstrate your skill level with the questionnaire. The HR specialist has the authority to reduce your score if the resume does not match the questionnaire answers.

Vacancy Announcement Example

KNOWLEDGE, SKILLS AND ABILITIES REQUIRED:

Your qualifications will be evaluated on the basis of your level of knowledge, skills, abilities and/or competencies in the following areas:

- Knowledge of the full range of principles and concepts of intelligence collection, analysis, evaluation, interpretation and dissemination of information.
- Knowledge of national intelligence community structure and responsibilities.
- Ability to perform extensive research to interpret intelligence data and present the results in customer usable form; and to analyze data and disseminate finished intelligence.
- Ability to operate laptop and desktop computers and peripherals including external hard drives, scanners, printers, CD/DVD recorders, network hub and switches, digital still and video cameras, global positioning systems and laser range finders.
- Skill in using and controlling classified data and equipment in accordance with established Department of Defense (DOD) security and classification guidelines and procedures.

HOW TO APPLY:

To apply for this position, you must provide a complete Application Package, which includes both of the following:

1. Your responses to the Qualifications Questionnaire, and

2. Your résumé and any other documents specified in the "Required Documents" section of this job announcement.

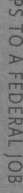

Adapting KSAs

There is no need to reinvent the wheel every time you submit a job application. If you save your KSAs in a word-processing application, you can access and edit them readily each time you prepare a new application. Often, an old KSA can be used again—either verbatim for a similar factor or adapted to a completely new one. Here is an example of one KSA used two ways. By changing the keywords and the important points of the examples, we can easily put a new slant on an old KSA. The edits between versions are illustrated so you can see how simple this is.

KSA version 1: Ability to communicate in writing.

My written communication skills are at an expert level as my abilities include presenting complex and technical issues clearly and concisely to diverse audiences of varied levels of understanding.

As a writer for the Correspondent Weekly (date - date), a regional political newspaper, I regularly wrote and edited stories on cultural and political topics of local and national interest, and ensured that issues were relevant and meaningful to a wide variety of audiences.

As an Assistant Multimedia Producer in the Corporate Headquarters of Campus Ministries International (date - date), I developed and wrote news stories, audio and video scripts, and talking points in English for a monthly, international satellite broadcast targeting 120 different nations, sometimes incorporating the organization's positions on various topics. I also served as a liaison for fellow staff members in the U.S. and overseas for ongoing audio and video multimedia projects, communicating with them in writing to convey important program information.

KSA version 2: Ability to proofread and ensure correct grammar, spelling, and punctuation.

My written communication skills are at an expert level ~~as my abilities include~~. I have had significant experience presenting complex and technical issues clearly and concisely to diverse audiences, each time ensuring correct grammar, spelling, and punctuation in order to maintain correct usage of language. ~~of varied levels of understanding.~~

As a writer for the Correspondent Weekly (date – date), a regional political newspaper, I regularly wrote and edited stories on cultural and political topics of local and national interest. Having responsibility for my work and ~~and ensured that issues were relevant and meaningful to a wide variety of audiences.~~ ensuring that deadlines were met without undue problems, I proofread my stories and ensured adherence to style and correctness, including punctuation and spelling.

As an Assistant Multimedia Producer in the Corporate Headquarters of Campus Ministries International (date - date), I developed and wrote news stories, audio and video scripts, and talking points in English for a monthly, international satellite broadcast targeting 120 different nations. Correct grammar, spelling, and punctuation were imperative to ensure flawless broadcasts and accurate information. I reviewed the work to ensure that all were correct before submitting stories for production. Because I ~~sometimes incorporating the organization's positions on various topics. I also~~ served as a liaison for fellow staff members in the U.S. and overseas for ongoing audio and video multimedia projects, ~~communicating with them in writing to convey important program information.~~ I frequently proofread the work of others as well.

Adapting KSAs: Long vs. Short KSAs

You can write long KSAs to prepare for the interview, but then edit the KSAs down to 300 or 400 characters to add them into your resume. We will use two KSAs from John Wallstone, our sous chef that we met in Steps 5 and 6. You will see these examples on the following pages.

CASE NAME: John Wallstone

PRIOR POSITION: Sous Chef, Executive Chef, Annapolis, MD

PAST SALARY: $60,000

TARGET FEDERAL JOB: Program Analyst, GS-0343-9/12

GENERAL ADMINISTRATIVE, CLERICAL, AND OFFICE SERVICES GROUP, GS-0300

John Wallstone KSA #1: Experience Managing Projects

LONGER VERSION FOR INTERVIEW PREP – 3,120 Characters

CONTEXT: Due to the nature of my career, I have had in-depth experience in leading projects requiring strong interpersonal, group and customer service skills. Kitchens are notorious for their abrasive relationships, which unfortunately can affect the customer; in my kitchens, I actively build solid teams with excellent communications, as well as work with my customers to ensure their satisfaction.

CHALLENGE: One of the largest events I have managed was a 425-person party, while at Government House. In addition to the size of the event, I had two other challenges – we were in the process of hiring a new manager and were presently short-staffed and another chef had a family emergency and took a leave of absence. Instead of three managers for the event, I had sole responsibility for it. I knew from the outset that I would need to recruit help from a variety of sources.

ACTIONS: Our lead time for the event was 10 days. In that period, I had to plan the menu, determine what items to order, recalculate recipes for mass production, determine what sequence to order and prep food, what items could be ordered pre-cut, what containers and serving items needed to be purchased and how to store and stage the product while avoiding contamination. (One challenge was receiving, storing and grilling 420 pounds of chicken, swordfish and pork.) During this process, I used object-oriented planning, working backwards from the final outcome to the initial step. Once the preplanning was completed, I began receiving products and commenced production.

In receiving the product, I had two major concerns: first were checks for quality, specifications, proper sanitation and avoiding cross-contamination, second was security. This event was about nine months after the 9/11 terrorist attacks. New security procedures had been implemented and the Maryland State Police had to be informed of incoming deliveries. To make special accommodations for the delivery, I worked with the MSP. I made sure detail leaders and commanders had delivery schedules and pertinent information, allowing us to successfully receive and house all products.

As the event approached, I began to recruit additional personnel. I brought in a retired chef for two days to help with production and a veteran chef for the day of the event. I also resolved problems that occurred, such as last-minute menu changes and coaching out of practice staff. I worked with my vendors to update my orders, oversaw the delivery and placement of a large rental grill and directed staff to pick up supplies.

RESULTS: As a result of my planning and problem resolution, the production, staging and eventual presentation of the food went smoothly. The event was a success; the guests and the client were very pleased. I demonstrated my skills as a planner, organizer, decision maker and crisis manager, solidifying my management's confidence in me as a project manager. The interruption of our staff by the chef's emergency absence was large enough to jeopardize the event's success. While the potential for widespread chaos existed, I brought a sense of calm, confidence and leadership to the situation.

SHORTER VERSION FOR QUESTIONNAIRES OR KSAS IN THE RESUME –
539 Characters

Managed a 425-person party, while in the process of hiring a new manager, short-staffed, family emergency for another chef, and just 10 days after 9/11 terrorists attacks. With lead time of 10 days, I planned the event. I used object-oriented planning, working backwards from the final outcome to the initial step. RESULTS: The event was a success; the guests and the client were very pleased. I demonstrated my skills as a planner, organizer, decision maker and crisis manager, solidifying my management's confidence in me as a project manager.

SHORTER VERSION FOR KSAS IN THE RESUME – 433 Characters

Managed a 425-person party, with staffing shortages just 10 days after 9/11 terrorist attacks. With lead time of 10 days, I used object-oriented planning, working backwards from the final outcome to the initial step. RESULTS: I demonstrated my skills as a planner, organizer, decision maker and crisis manager, solidifying my management's confidence in me as a project manager. The event was a success; the guests and the client were very pleased.

John Wallstone KSA #2: Demonstrated Ability to Work Effectively in a Team Environment and Interact with Internal and External Customers

LONGER VERSION FOR INTERVIEW PREP – 3,942 Characters

In many work environments, establishing and maintaining effective working relationships is key to success. In my own experience, I have found this to be particularly true. As such, it is a major part of my management (and work) strategy to build relationships across organizational and agency barriers, working with a wide range of internal and external customers and staff to run successful organizations.

CONTEXT / CHALLENGE: When I first started at Government House, communications between departments and in the kitchen were abysmal. By nature of the assignment, there should have been interaction between all groups operating and working with Government House – kitchen staff, Maryland State Troopers, executive staff, legislative staff and Department of General Services staff, at all staff levels. Instead, animosity had built up between staffs and older employees conditioned new employees to be leery of interacting with Government House staff. The result was uncooperative territorialism. Cooperation and teamwork were nearly non-existent.

ACTIONS: Recognizing the problem, I made a direct effort to change the environment, using my interpersonal and communications skills to make the office more open and cooperative. If I learned information the troopers could use, I shared it with them. For example, if I learned that Governor Ehrlich was going to deviate from his schedule during his meeting with the kitchen staff, I informed the troopers. This process was slow to start, as I had to prove myself trustworthy and undo the "us versus them" mentality. In staff meetings and by my own example, I stressed teamwork. For example, if I received a financial request from the Governor's Office, I always attempted to go above and beyond the request. I gave them the most accurate information and in a timely manner, with professional documents and information on how to merge it with their reports. Information has included inventory, menu calculation, consumption, number of parties held and client demographics.

I have worked to make the various staffs feel welcome in Government House, interacting with them in a friendly manner and keeping my word to build trust. I have nurtured an open, cooperative, team-first relationship. For the troopers, I make an effort to tailor their meals to their liking and provide extras to make their days easier, such as beverages, snacks and supplies to demonstrate good will. For the executive staff, I participate in press appearances, briefings, event planning and budget reporting. During my tenure, I have worked for both Democratic and Republican governors and have established effective working relationships with both.

With kitchen staff, I have worked to eliminate the "I don't need help" approach, instead emphasizing teamwork. During staff meetings, I encourage staff members to communicate and call for help early. This approach was new to many of the workers. Once staff members realized asking for help was a good decision, instead of a sign of weakness, we experienced better staff communication and higher morale. Additionally, I am willing to take on extra responsibility to help others. I often run errands, help unload products and help others with their duties. This has strengthened my working relationship with the other members of our staff and built trust.

RESULTS: Since instituting my team-first approach and actively building relationships, the atmosphere at Government House is improved on many levels. Our flow of information and cooperation has increased tremendously. The hoarding of information as a source of power has been eliminated and animosity and control issues have diminished. I have shown we can work together without compromising privacy, security and operational integrity. Most importantly, the staffs know they can trust that I am on their side and will help where and when I can. The final result of this improved relationship is better service to the First Family and more efficient operations.

SHORTER VERSION FOR QUESTIONNAIRES OR KSAS IN THE RESUME –
726 Characters

When I first started at Government House, communications between State Troopers (security) departments and in the kitchen were abysmal. I made a direct effort to change the environment, using my interpersonal and communications skills to make the office more open and cooperative. If I learned information the troopers could use, I shared it with them. Information has included inventory, menu calculation, consumption, number of parties held and client demographics. RESULTS: Since instituting my team-first approach and actively building relationships, the atmosphere at Government House is improved on many levels. The final result of this improved relationship is better service to the First Family and more efficient operations.

SHORTER VERSION FOR KSAS IN THE RESUME – 537Characters

Improved communications between the State Troopers (security) departments and the kitchen. If I learned information the troopers could use, I shared it with them. Information has included inventory, menu calculation, consumption, number of parties held and client demographics. RESULTS: Since instituting my team-first approach and actively building relationships, the atmosphere at Government House is improved on many levels. The final result of this improved relationship is better service to the First Family and more efficient operations.

SHORTER VERSION FOR KSAS IN THE RESUME – 299 Characters

Improved communications between the State Troopers (security) departments and the kitchen. Shared event information, including client demographics. RESULTS: Since instituting my team-first approach and actively building relationships, improved service to the First Family and more efficient operations.

Writing the Impossible KSA

Every now and then you may come across a KSA in a vacancy announcement that you feel you just cannot write. You are a great fit for the job, but there is one KSA that just stumps you. You have no experience in that area, or perhaps you have never even heard of the program, system, or regulation. Before you give up, consider this.

You can write a truthful, on-target, and effective KSA for the stumper. How? By looking to other areas of your life experience for examples, drawing parallels to what you do know or performing your own research to learn about that KSA. Obviously, you do not want to lie in your answer. You cannot manufacture knowledge, skills, and abilities that you do not have. But telling the reviewer what you know and how you know it can fulfill the KSA and keep you on track as an excellent candidate.

"After our discussion, I realized that many of the responses [where] I rated myself lower would be at the expert level since people have come to me for assistance on these items. Even when the question refers to very specific reports or unit procedures, there is usually a private industry parallel for it that I have experienced. I do understand that if I respond at an expert level, I need to make sure these are clearly identifiable in my resume to validate my responses."
--John Naperkoski

Knowledge KSA from Life Experience

In this KSA example, the applicant had personal experience from interactions that were not part of her work experience. This is a valid experience for the KSA factor and counts toward the qualifications for the job. While she may not score as high as someone with direct work experience in this area, she will earn points for her explanation, and along with her other strong KSAs, she has a good shot at the job.

Prior Position: IT Specialist
Target Federal Job: Centers for Medicare & Medicaid Services, Health Insurance Specialist, GS-0107-12
KSA Factor: Knowledge of needs and preferences of people who are elderly or have a chronic illness or disability.

Response

Much of my knowledge of the needs and preferences of people who are elderly or have a chronic illness or disability is the result of personal experiences. As the primary caregiver for my blind, severely disabled elderly sister for the past ten years, I have personal, firsthand knowledge of the needs and preferences of people with chronic illness and disability. And while "book knowledge" is valuable as a facts resource, there is no better teacher than living and caring for a disabled loved-one 24/7, 365 days a year.

Experiencing firsthand the responsibilities of caring for a disabled relative has not only provided me with a knowledge of their needs and preferences, but it has also given me a thorough understanding of what a family experiences when negotiating the maze of health care services. As a result of my experiences, I am very familiar with the insurance and Medicare/Medicaid services that are available to individuals with special needs, as well as those that are not.

I have helped my sister secure coverage under the Medicare and Medicaid programs. I have a thorough knowledge and understanding of the eligibility requirements, coverage for Part A and Part B, and premium payments, as well as the HMO and Private Fee for Service Plans. I coordinate all of her health care and her personal care.

My first-hand knowledge of the needs and preferences of those with chronic illnesses or disability, coupled with previous career experience in the health insurance industry, have provided me with the knowledge base to analyze and understand new information quickly and easily. Whenever I encounter something I do not know, I research materials and resources available or find someone who can share their knowledge so that I can find the best solution to the problem. I am never afraid to ask for guidance, because that is often the best way to gain a better understanding of a subject and learn new information.

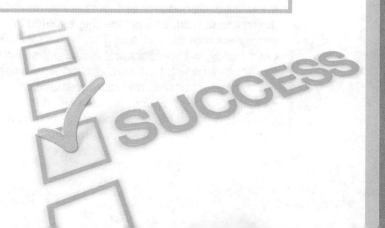

Knowledge KSA from a Parallel Knowledge

Describing how you did what was asked is a great way to show your competence. In this example, an attorney practiced land use and environmental law in Florida, but the issues were different in Colorado, where he was applying. He demonstrated his skills and knowledge with examples from his experience and stated his familiarity with the specific laws in the KSA.

Prior Position: Private Practice Attorney (Solo Practitioner)
Target Federal Job: Department of the Interior, Attorney-Advisor and General Attorney, GS-905-14/15
KSA Factor: Experience with resource laws administered by the Department, e.g. National Environmental Policy Act, the Mineral Leasing Act Federal Land Policy and Management Act and Endangered Species Act. Provide examples of the issues you have reviewed for legal sufficiency and compliance with applicable case law and/or regulations and the outcome.

Response

A specialty throughout my legal career has been in governmental law with an emphasis on land use law and development. In that capacity I have represented numerous governmental entities including St. Johns County, Florida; the Supervisor of Elections, various cities (conflict cases), and numerous fire and water districts. In so doing, I have reviewed and approved a myriad of documents (contracts, leases, memorandums, etc.).

CONTEXT: I have represented many people before the government who were either opposed or in favor of a land use decision. Invariably this involved working with highly trained professionals such as architects, engineers, planners, environmentalists, and the like. Many of the environmental issues at hand involved surface water management, exotics, wildlife habitats, endangered species, loss of wetlands, and the mining of phosphate minerals. In Florida where I practiced, issues were governed by state resource and land management laws, protected wetlands, and endangered species, among other resources. For example, if a development had an area wherein there lived endangered species such as a gopher tortoise nest, this had to be preserved. Additionally, if a wetland was permitted to be destroyed then at least twice as much wetland or more had to be preserved. These were the environmental issues in my neck of the woods.

CHALLENGE: In one particular case, the government was exacting land to be used for a frontage road from a small church. ACTIONS: My client, the church, merely wanted to build a small school addition to its church and it happened to be in front of an arterial road. The government denied the permit unless they provided a frontage road to alleviate traffic. We went through the administrative appeals process and simultaneously sued, claiming that the exaction violated the due process and eminent domain clauses of the constitution.

RESULTS: In this reported case, the appellate court held that the government could not use the permitting process as a means of "land banking". The outcome caused not only the small church to proceed, but caused the return of numerous lands "banked" by the government. I am familiar with the resource laws administered by the Department of the Interior such as the National Environmental Policy Act, the Mineral Leasing Act, the Federal Land Policy and Management Act, and the Endangered Species Act. I am knowledgeable of the issues to which these are applied such as endangered species (e.g. osprey and eagle nests, gopher tortoise, and manatee habitats, et al in Florida), environmental habitats (e.g. wetlands, cypress sloughs, et al in Florida), and various solutions, such as conservation easements within the development or purchase of multiple acres per acre of wetlands outside of the development to be deeded to the government.

Knowledge KSA from Education

Describing your relevant coursework and featuring accomplishments, awards, and good performance in an academic environment are valid experiences from which to draw for a knowledge KSA. In this case, there is not one CCAR example to describe; therefore a list of the candidate's experiences that illustrates what she achieved is given instead.

Past Position: Masters Student and Library Intern
Target Position: Library of Congress, Library Technician, GS 7/8
KSA Factor: Knowledge of the history and literature of music.

Response

I have a stellar educational background in the history and literature of music. I graduated magna cum laude from Ministry College in 20xx with a Bachelor of Arts degree, majoring in Music. The music program at Ministry College is history and literature based. To further develop my knowledge of music as well as complement this degree, I completed the Joint-Degree Program in Music Librarianship at American Christian University in 20xx. As such, I received both a Master of Science in Library Science and a Master of Arts in Musicology.

As a graduate student, I completed 57 credits in the joint-degree graduate program in a period of 23 months, essentially completing a three-year program in two years. Due to my command of the French language, I passed the language requirement before I began my graduate studies. Furthermore, I passed the Library Science and Musicology comprehensive exams the first time I took them. The graduate courses demanded thorough analysis of musical sources and a wide knowledge of music literature. My coursework included Renaissance, Romantic, and 20th-century music, including a seminar on song cycles. All of these courses were based on the history and literature of music. Throughout my program I developed a passion for learning about the role woman composers play in music history and I elected to focus my research on women composers in all of the aforementioned courses.

While studying Music at Ministry College, I took courses in music history ranging from Medieval music to music of the 20th century. I also took a specialized course in Rhythm-and-Blues, as well as a seminar in World music. I gained practical knowledge while singing with the Ministry College Chorale for four years. The repertoire included challenging works by classical composers which reinforced my study of music history and literature.
I also sang with the Collegium Musicum, an ensemble dedicated to the interpretation and performance of early music. Additionally, I studied both solo voice (specializing in classical art songs, particularly those by women composers) and classical piano with private teachers.

As a result of the attention I pay to my studies and the growth and development of my career, I have an excellent understanding of music history, as well as an exceptional ability to research and use information resources. I was awarded the Mollie Seltzer Yett Prize for Excellence in Music Academics in recognition of my knowledge and abilities. As a result of my interest in women composers at American Christian University, I developed a research paper on the vocal music of Clara Schumann, the wife of Robert Schumann and a composer in her own right. The research paper was selected from many entries to be presented at the Spring 20xx meeting of the Atlantic Chapter of the Society of Music History, and I received the first place prize of $250.

STEP EIGHT
Apply for Jobs

How Many Applications Will I Need to Submit?

There are about 30,000 to 40,000 open positions posted on USAJOBS every day. An average federal applicant might apply to 20 to 50 positions over a period of four to six months. If your resume is targeted toward a particular federal job title and the correct grade or salary level, it is possible to apply to ten jobs and get Best Qualified and Referred for most of them. However, I have also seen applicants apply to 200 jobs without even getting Minimally Qualified for a position. Avoid the major pitfalls by following the proven strategies in this book! In this particular step, the major key to successfully applying for a federal job is to carefully follow every instruction regarding your application submission.

Package What They Want

Online Applications: For online applications, complete all of the pages and questions. Make sure you finish the submission. Sometimes there are at least four steps to applying: Profile/ Registration; Resume Builder; Questions or Essays; and document upload. For the resume builder, be sure you do not exceed the maximum number of characters allowed in a field. Follow the outline format federal resume for easy reading—see the sample in Step 6.

Do not use the Resume Upload feature. USAJOBS gives you the option of uploading your paper resume, but I don't recommend that you do this. It is better to copy and paste your resume content into the Resume Builder, which will prompt you to include important information such as: month and year of employers; hours per week for each position for the last 10 years; supervisor's name and phone; address for employers. The Resume Upload also has had some problems being forwarded into questionnaire systems or other online application systems.

Combination Online and Fax: When you apply online, you may be asked to fax additional information, such as a copy of your transcripts, veterans documents, Schedule A Letter (for persons with disabilities), or performance evaluation. Make sure you use the designated fax cover sheet. Include your Social Security Number (last four digits), name, and announcement number on each page submitted by fax.

Paper Packages: The appearance of your application is important. If you are applying via a paper package, use good quality bond paper. White is customary, but you may use ivory colored paper. Your cover letter, resume, and KSAs should be separate documents. Transcripts can be photocopies and do not need to be official copies. Package your documents in a large envelope so that they do not have to be folded. Do not staple pages together. For paper applications, you may be asked to submit multiple copies. Always comply with the instructions.

Read the "How To Apply" Instructions

To apply for a federal position, read the instructions on the "How to Apply" tab of the announcement on USAJOBS or other agency website. Since each agency or department of the federal government is a separate entity, each agency may have a slightly different application requirement to apply for positions. The "how to apply" page is critical to the success of your federal job campaign. On that page you will find out what will be required to actually apply for the position.

Beware and be calm: the instructions are slightly unique on most of the announcements. This is a TEST to see if you can FOLLOW DIRECTIONS. Read this page and the Qualifications page CAREFULLY to get all of the instructions. Here are some of the typical combinations of instructions you will find:

✪ Submit your resume to USAJOBS.gov, complete the Questionnaire on applicationmanager. org, and upload PDFs or files of transcripts, DD-214, or other documents online.

✪ Submit your resume to CPOL.army.mil with KSAs covered in the resume. Complete the Self-Nomination form to actually apply for the position.

✪ DO NOT SUBMIT YOUR RESUME TO USAJOBS. Go to avuecentral.com to create your resume in the builder at that site. Complete the questionnaire at avuecentral.com. Upload other documents into avuecentral.com

✪ Submit your resume into CHART, the U.S. Navy and USMC resume builder and application website. Set up a profile and then complete the Self-Nomination form. NOTE: Both Army CPOL and Navy CHART systems will be eliminated in the next year. You should submit on both CPOL and USAJOBS to make sure your resume is ready in USAJOBS when CPOL is eliminated.

Each resume builder has its own Applicant Profile, so you will create an account on all of the builders: USAJOBS, applicationmanager.org, CPOL, Avue, CHART, WHS, and/or agency-specific websites that are of interest to you.

Strategy Tips

Be sure to check off Permanent, Term, and Temp for all builders, so you will be considered for all kinds of positions.

Keep a log of your passwords and login information for each system. For some agencies, you cannot reset a lost password automatically and may not be able to get the assistance you need before your vacancy deadline.

Resume Builder Chart

Name of Agency	Agency Jobs Website	Automated Recruitment System	Question-naire
Agriculture	http://www.usda.gov/da/employ/director.htm	USAJOBS / Applicationmanager	Yes
Air Force Civilian Personnel	http://www.afciviliancareers.com/index.php	USAJOBS / Applicationmanager	Yes
US Army Civilian Personnel	http://www.cpol.army.mil	CPOL/Resumix	No
Bureau of Land Management	http://www.blm.gov/jobs/	USAJOBS / Applicationmanager	Yes
Central Intelligence Agency	https://www.cia.gov/careers/index.html	CIA Builder	No
Citizenship & Immigration	http://www.uscis.gov/	USAJOBS / Applicationmanager	Yes
Commerce	http://www.commerce.gov/about-commerce/careers	USAJOBS / Monster	Yes
Customs & Border Protection	http://www.cbp.gov/xp/cgov/careers/	USAJOBS / Applicationmanager	Yes
Defense Contract Management Agency	http://www.dcma.mil/careers/index.cfm	Army Resumix	No
Defense Finance and Accounting Office	http://www.dod.mil/dfas/careers.html	USAJOBS / Applicationmanager	Yes
Defense Logistics Agency	http://www.dla.mil/careers.aspx	USAJOBS / Applicationmanager	Yes
Environmental Protection Agency	http://www.epa.gov/careers/	USAJOBS/ Monster	Yes
FAA	http://www.faa.gov/jobs/	Aviator	Yes
FBI	http://www.fbijobs.gov	FBIJOBS, QuickHire	Yes
FEMA	http://www.fema.gov/career	USAJOBS / Applicationmanager	Yes
Forest Service	http://www.fs.fed.us/fsjobs/	Avuecentral.com	Yes
General Accountability Office	http://www.gao.gov/careers/index.html	USAJOBS	Yes
General Services Administration	http://www.gsa.gov (GSA Careers link on right)	GSA Jobs	Yes
HHS Careers	http://www.hhs.gov/careers/	USAJOBS / Applicationmanager	Yes
Health & Human Services	http://www.hhs.gov/careers	HHS Careers/USAJOBS	Yes
HHS National Institutes of Health	http://www.training.nih.gov/careers/careercenter	NIH/HHS Careers / USAJOBS	Yes
Homeland Security	http://www.dhs.gov/xabout/careers	USAJOBS	Yes

Name of Agency	Agency Jobs Website	Automated Recruitment System	Question-naire
Housing and Urban Development	http://www.hud.gov/jobs/index.cfm	USAJOBS / Applicationmanager	Yes
Interior	http://www.doi.gov/employees/index.cfm	USAJOBS / Applicationmanager	Yes
Justice	http://www.justice.gov/careers/careers.html	Avue Central	Yes
NASA	http://www.nasajobs.nasa.gov/	USAJOBS / Applicationmanager	Yes
Navy Civilian Personnel CHART	https://www.donhr.navy.mil/	Navy CHART/Resumix	No
Defense, Office of the Secretary	http://www.defense.gov/osd/	USAJOBS / Applicationmanager	Yes
Peace Corps	http://www.avuecentral.com	Avue Central	Yes
Small Business Administration	http://www.sba.gov	USAJOBS / Applicationmanager	Yes
State Department	http://careers.state.gov/	USAJOBS / Gateway to State	Yes
Transportation	http://careers.dot.gov/	USAJOBS/Monster	Yes
Transportation Security Agency	http://www.tsa.gov/join/careers/	TSO Application / Monster	Yes
US Marshal's Service	http://www.justice.gov/marshals/careers/index.html	Avue Central	Yes
Veterans Administration	http://www.va.gov/jobs/	USAJOBS / Applicationmanager	Yes

Disclaimer: Research for this spreadsheet was completed on early 2011. Please know that resume builders, agency career website addresses, methods of collecting resumes, and other information may change from week to week. We will attempt to stay up-to-date by posting this spreadsheet at www.resume-place.com. Please write builders@resume-place.com for updates that you may have found.

Tips: Writing for a Resume Builder

1. Read specific instructions for each resume builder.

2. If your electronic resume is longer than the resume builder character requirements, the extraneous characters could be cut off.

3. Be sure to format your electronic resume to be compatible with the builder. You cannot copy and paste a resume with formatting (bold type, bullets, indentations, etc.) into a builder. The resume will possibly be unreadable and could be rejected.

4. Create your resume in a word processing program in order to check for spelling and grammar mistakes. This is also a helpful way to store your documents from which you can cut and paste, as builders time out. All content should be composed in a word processing program, saved there, and then transferred over. Paste or type your information into each block, as you want it to appear on the resume. Many of the builders allow hard returns to leave blank lines between paragraphs.

5. In the USAJOBS resume builder, you CAN use bullets if you copy and paste them from Microsoft Word. You can see the bullets for accomplishments in our sample in Step 6. Be sure to PREVIEW your resume to check the formatting. The Army CPOL builder (which will be retired soon) does not accept bullets. In fact, the CPOL builder won't even accept an asterisk or apostrophe, so do not use any possessive words in that builder. Count characters in your job blocks and other categories based on the resume builder instructions. You can either use Word Count from the Tools menu in Microsoft Word or cut and paste it into the actual Resume Builder to get the most accurate count. Make sure you count the spaces.

6. Periodically save your resume as you enter it into the builder to avoid losing your information in the event you get timed out.

Tips: Keeping Character Count Under Control

1. Use acronyms, but carefully. Write out the entire phrase first, then use the acronym. Remember that the HR specialists need to understand what you are writing.

2. Use one space between sentences instead of two.

3. Cut transitional or introductory words that you do not need, like the word "that" used earlier in this sentence.

4. Use short words like "use" instead of long ones like "utilize." Make this a habit.

5. Edit your KSA accomplishments down to the most important sentences. Unless you really need to know a detail to understand the accomplishment, cut it.

Avoiding Application Pitfalls & Other Tips

✪ If the position is an Army position, you MUST apply with your resume in the CPOL builder.

✪ If the position is a Navy position, you MUST apply with your resume in the CHART builder.

✪ If the position is managed and recruited by Avue Central, you must submit and apply directly to Avue Central.

✪ If the position is managed by OPM, and they are using USAJOBS and Application Manager, then you must hit SUBMIT in the system to actually apply for a position.

✪ If the announcement states that you MUST submit additional documents into the system, you MUST do that.

✪ If the announcement states that you must use THEIR fax cover, then you MUST do that.

✪ If you submit your username and password to USAJOBS incorrectly three times, you will be locked out. It's easy to reset your password, and it just takes a few minutes.

✪ You can only have one resume in the Army, Navy, and Washington Headquarter Services (WHS) builders at one time. You will have to change keywords carefully to submit resumes for announcements with close dates.

✪ USAJOBS builder allows you to select Confidential. Do not select Confidential or the supervisor will not be able to see your past employers.

✪ You MUST hit the SUBMIT, APPLY, or SEND buttons in the various builders. Otherwise, you will not have applied to any job.

✪ The USAJOBS builder gives you the SAVE option at the bottom of the page ONLY. If you GO BACK with content on that page that is not saved, it will be lost.

✪ The USAJOBS builder gives you 3,000 characters (including spaces) for each job. If your current job is longer than 3,000 characters, you can continue that description in the second job block.

✪ USAJOBS resumes are viewable by some federal agency managers and all human resources specialists. The USAJOBS resumes are also now searchable by HR recruiters, and this resume search sytem is sometimes used by agencies. Be sure to name your resume in the USAJOBS builder appropriately for the application, such as: SBA Administrative Officer, GS 9; NCIS Program Analyst, GS12; FBI Information Technology Specialist (Customer Services), GS 12; or Intelligence Analyst, GS-13.

How to Apply: USAJOBS

USAJOBS allows a jobseeker to have up to five versions of the resume in the database at once. This makes focusing your resume on a particular job series very easy. You can update your resumes in USAJOBS as often as you like. It is a rigid format; for example, you do not have the flexibility to list education before experience or put your work experience out of chronological order.

Putting a resume in USAJOBS does not mean that you have applied to a job; you are simply storing your resume in the database for later use. You must click "APPLY ONLINE" to start an actual application.

For some announcements, the USAJOBS resume, along with the supplemental data section, is the whole application. For others, the USAJOBS resume is used in tandem with another online system or faxed documents. Follow each step in sequence until you receive a confirmation that your application was sent.

TIPS:

Put your resume into the USAJOBS online database BEFORE starting an application. Name each of your resumes (up to five) with a specific job title, grade and agency, in case an HR recruiter searches the database for titles or keywords for positions.

Step by Step: USAJOBS Resume and Application

1. Create a USAJOBS account and fill in your profile information.

2. Use the resume builder in "MY USAJOBS" to create your federal resume. There are many sections to fill in besides work experience and education. Provide as much information as you can that will show your qualifications for the job. You can have up to five different versions in the system at once.

3. Find your announcement and determine whether you can apply by checking the "Who May Be Considered" section.

4. After your resume is in the system, click "Apply Online" to start the application process.

5. USAJOBS will ask you which version of your resume you want to use for that particular application. Select the one targeted for that job.

6. If the application requires you to complete information on an additional website, your browser will take you there.

7. Follow all steps through final submission.

USAJOBS Resume Builder – Five Resumes

Different set of keywords? Create different resumes in USAJOBS. You can store up to five different resumes on USAJOBS. If you analyze your keywords for more than one job series, you might want to have different resume versions naming the resume with that job title. The sample below is for the author of this book. She would have different keywords for each resume.

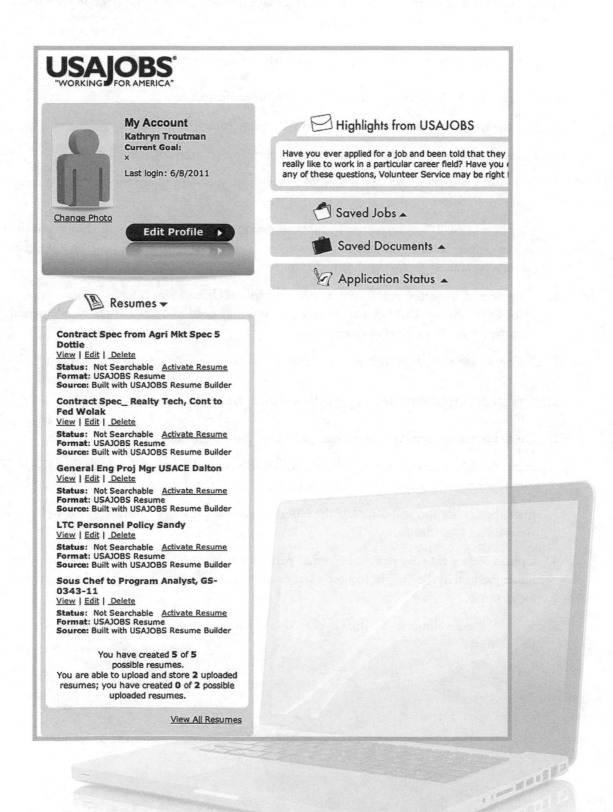

How to Apply: USA Staffing Application Manager

This automated system is frequently used in conjunction with USAJOBS, where https://applicationmanager.gov is the utility for administering the self-assessment and supplemental data questions. You can pull your resume from the USAJOBS online database, or you can upload your resume file. The upload allows greater flexibility in your resume presentation because you can format it however you like.

Step by step: Application Manager with USAJOBS Resume Retrieval

1. Create a USAJOBS account and fill in your profile information.

2. Use the resume builder in "My USAJOBS" to create your federal resume.

3. Find your announcement and click "Apply Online" to start the application process.

4. USAJOBS will ask you which version of your resume you want to use for that particular application. Select the one targeted for that job.

5. Your browser will then direct you to applicationmanager.gov to complete the biographical and eligibility information and start the Assessment Questionnaire. You will see that you must create a separate login for Application Manager.

6. Complete all questions and follow all steps including "Upload Documents." You will not upload a resume or KSA documents, however, you may need to upload or fax supplemental documents like transcripts or veterans forms.

7. Follow all steps through "Submit My Answers," or your application will not be submitted.

Step by step: Application Manager with Resume Upload

1. Go to https://applicationmanager.org and create your login and Profile.

2. Enter the job announcement number or USAJOBS control number (found in the USAJOBS vacancy announcement) to retrieve your target vacancy application.

3. Start the application and complete the biographical and eligibility information as well as the Assessment Questionnaire.

4. Upload and/or fax your resume and other pertinent application documents as well as other information that they might request—last evaluation, DD-214 (veterans), and transcripts, for example.

5. Follow all steps through "SUBMIT MY ANSWERS," or your application will not be submitted.

How to Apply: AvueCentral.com

This commercial system is used by more than 12 agencies, including the USAID, Library of Congress, Peace Corps, and Millennium Challenge Corporation. This application is a complex online form with questions and a profile. You submit your resume one time, and then apply for one or more positions in the database that Avue Central maintains. However, this can only be done for vacancies in agencies using this system.

Most jobs posted on AvueCentral.com are also posted on USAJOBS. That means that you can search for them in USAJOBS, where there is greater search flexibility and ease of use, and then apply to them through AvueCentral.com as instructed. You can go to AvueCentral.com directly; however, it is often easier to access the application by starting in USAJOBS and clicking "Apply Online."

Step by step: Avue Central

1. From the USAJOBS vacancy, click "Apply Online" and your browser will direct you to that particular vacancy in AvueCentral.com or you can go directly to the Avue Central home page and search for the vacancy.

2. Log on or create your Profile in AvueCentral.com. Click "Apply Now" to start the application process.

3. On the left side of the screen, you will see a menu for filling in Mandatory Information, such as your work history, education, and KSAs. The application will automatically pull your resume information from your Profile; however, you also have the option to revise it for the particular application.

4. Each vacancy announcement in Avue Central has "Job Posting Information" that includes the description that you saw posted in USAJOBS as well as the actual Position Description. Use this information to write your resume content (keywords).

5. Once you have completed every section in Mandatory Information, click "Send Application" to complete the process.

Tip:

Some online builders and applications have places to indicate your race, national origin, gender, or medical/disability information. This information is NOT required and it will not adversely affect your application if you decline to answer.

How to Apply: U.S. Navy's CHART or Army's CPOL

The Army CPOL and Navy CHART systems are both keyword systems. The human resources specialist will search for the best qualified people based on keywords that are found in either the vacancy announcement or other sources (as described in Step 4, Find the Perfect Job Announcement).

NOTE: Both of these systems are scheduled endin 2011. Please submit your resume to USAJOBS as well when you apply through CHART or CPOL.

Open Continuously – Inventory Building – Database Building Announcements. The Navy announcements have very short "duty" descriptions and list multiple job titles in an occupational series. These are databases where HR professionals will search for qualified candidates when positions become available. These are valuable and real announcements. If you are qualified for these positions you should submit your resume to these databases.

The Army announcements have excellent descriptions of duties and specialized experience. You can find a good keyword description in Army announcements.

Self-Nomination Process

If your resume is already in the database, you can simply "self-nominate" for a special position that interests you. The Navy uses both Open Continuously announcements and special announcements with closing dates. You will not need to resend or resubmit your resume to the particular database. Make sure your resume is in the right database.

Step by Step: CHART or CPOL

1. Create a profile in the pertinent system and fill in your biographical and supplemental data information.

2. Write the correct length resume paying special attention to whether your content fits within the character limitations.

3. Paste your resume into the online system ahead of the deadline. Sometimes there are special instructions about how far in advance your resume needs to be submitted.

4. Self-nominate for the job according to the agency's instructions.

5. The Supplemental Data Sheet is now part of the Builder and you will complete it online. This is very important in that it shows your eligibility for certain jobs based on whether you have status.

Cover Letters

You might think that cover letters do not have a place in our online application world. But in fact, the Federal Hiring Reform implemented in November 2010 stated that you could use a resume and cover letter as your application. A cover letter can be uploaded into USAJOBS and Application Manager, and this additional piece of your application is another invaluable way to market yourself. You can effectively use the cover letter to present your unique experiences that not only show how you qualify for the job, but also why you are the best candidate for the job.

In business, any good sales pitch does not just tell the features and benefits of a product one time. It repeats the selling points several times, reviewing features and benefits, giving a demonstration, and then telling the customer how the product will help them achieve their goals. A good federal application package uses sales repetition about your qualifications for the job in this way:

1. Federal Resume and KSA Accomplishments – presents detailed work experience, education, specialized experience, and examples

2. Questionnaires – demonstrates your highest level of experience

3. Cover Letter – summarizes your best qualifications and how you will benefit the organization

What a Persuasive Cover Letter Can Do

A great cover letter is simply one that creates an impression of you. It directs your reader's attention by showcasing your professionalism. It points out your best traits. Also, the letter can personalize your application package. It is a wonderful chance for you to speak directly to your reader, the hiring supervisor. It is your chance for you to say, "Hey, look at me! I'm the best-qualified, most interesting candidate. Call me!"

Like a goodwill ambassador, a strong cover letter can greet the reader who picks up your application, casting a positive light on you at a critical point in the application process. This letter can impart your passion for the work or the agency's mission and be an enthusiastic voice for your qualifications. Use the cover letter to:

- ✪ Summarize the best you have to offer
- ✪ Write about your interests or passions in a particular field or job
- ✪ Highlight your expertise and qualifications that specifically fit the job
- ✪ Demonstrate your knowledge of the agency's mission
- ✪ Showcase your value as an employee
- ✪ Create a compelling rationale for why you are an outstanding candidate

Draft your cover letter with our online template, used successfully by thousands of job seekers at http://www.resume-place.com/fedres_builder/cover_letter.

Recommended Cover Letter Structure

A solid cover letter is a one-page document with four main elements—each assigned a paragraph in the letter.

Paragraph #1: Explain what you are submitting and why

For example: "I am submitting the enclosed resume and KSA set as my application for the position of Public Health Advisor with the National Safety Council." Be sure to reference the job announcement number so that it can be matched to the rest of your application. If you have special or unusual circumstances for seeking the job, explain them here.

Paragraph #2: My relevant qualifications include...

In this paragraph, present your qualifications either in narrative (paragraph) form or as bulleted points. Read the vacancy to discern the top skills and use those as a guide for how to organize your summary of experience in the cover letter. This is the best way to show why YOU are the best candidate for the job. It DEMONSTRATES that your qualifications match the needs of the position.

Paragraph #3: I would be an asset to your organization because...

Think about the top three to five skills the supervisor is seeking. Think about what you can do to help that supervisor achieve their mission goals. Put yourself inside your reader's head and consider what in your background would make them sit up and take notice of your qualifications. You can use core competencies in this section. For example:

"I have a proven track record of leading enterprise level projects and programs requiring IT investment management, architecture implementation, and policy compliance."

"I am enthusiastic and flexible, with the ability to travel without limitation on short notice for my job. Because of my excellent physical fitness, I possess great energy and work well in high-pressure environments."

"My work experience in print and online media has keenly developed my ability to work effectively as part of a team."

Paragraph #4: Offer to come in for an interview and offer logistics information

For example: "I am available to meet with you at your convenience to discuss your objectives and my background. You can contact me at either telephone number above. Thank you for your time and consideration. I look forward to your response."

Closing/signature

Use a standard business closing and signature. However, list all of the enclosures you are submitting with your application, including your federal resume, KSA narratives, college transcripts, and anything else required in your application. For example:

Sincerely,
Helen R. Waters
Enclosures:

Explain Special Accommodations Needed for Disabilities

At this time, there is a special hiring initiative for hiring people with disabilities, so if you have a disability, you should try to apply for positions in government and indicate your disability in your cover letter.

Sample introductory paragraph for a cover letter to the Selective Placement Program Coordinator, Human Resources Specialist or Manager for a Schedule A application:

> I am writing to introduce my skills and experience for positions with your agency. I am a person with a disability and a Schedule A Letter. I am employment ready and have outstanding skills and abilities in the areas of customer services, computer skills, data, and information management. I would like to be considered for positions as Administrative Assistant or Management Assistant, GS-301- 7/9. My resume demonstrates that I have the specialized experience for this series and grade. Please consider my resume and refer my request to supervisors in your agency.

This one-page letter should include highlights of your experience, education, and maybe one short accomplishment.

Paragraph about accommodations: Discuss your disability and let them know about the accommodations you will need for your best job performance. Sample text:

> I am a person with a 90% visual disability. In order to perform effectively in my position, I would simply need special software on the computer so that I could listen to my email and other data. I have excellent health and hearing capabilities, so I am a high-performing employee with the exception of sight capability. I travel easily with a cane and learn new physical environments very quickly. I have a positive attitude and am willing to work hard and learn new policies, procedures, and programs.

It is your decision whether you will write about your disability and special accommodations in your initial application. Keep in mind, though, that agencies do have resources to help such individuals with special software, hardware, and physical accommodations so that they can have a meaningful, well-paid position. The federal government is hiring people with disabilities!

Discuss with your State Rehabilitation Specialist, job search counselor, and your family how you might communicate your particular strengths and your special needs. This is a personal decision, whether to tell the potential hiring manager about your disability or not. Nevertheless, the federal government is mandated to hire thousands of employees with disabilities in the next few years.

Special Emphasis Officers—human resources staff—are tasked with finding qualified, skilled people with disabilities to hire into positions that can accommodate special needs employees. If you are working through a State Rehab Counselor, obtain a Schedule A letter stating that you have a disability. Then you can seek a position in government without going through the "competitive process" of writing KSAs and applying for announced positions. It could be important to tell the Special Emphasis Officer and Hiring Supervisor of your disability and your strengths, skills, and interest in working for the federal government.

Public service agencies have excellent job opportunities for all people—those with and without disabilities. However, hiring managers and personnel staff need to know the special accommodations that you will require to determine if the job will work for your skills and abilities.

Cover Letter Sample

Deborah Thomas
34578 Harwell Court
Bethesda, MD 21228
Phone: 301-555-5555
Email: dthomas@email.com

July 21, 20xx

Internal Revenue Service
Attn: Sharla Houston
5555 Garden Road
Memphis, TN 38118

Dear Ms. Houston:

Enclosed is my application responding to **Vacancy Announcement #81ME-1-BM08-14-CH, Management Program Analyst**. I have included my federal resume, KSA narratives, and other requested documentation which highlight my professional experience and relevant accomplishments over the past ten years. I currently live in an area commutable to D.C.

I can offer the **Small Business/Self-Employed Business Unit** of the IRS proven Project Management experience. I have a successful track record in specialized, technical human resources management in these five areas:

- More than 11 years experience in executive positions in human resources with a focus on **leadership coaching and development**.

- Proven expertise in developing and managing **human resources policies** and procedures for dynamically changing organizations.

- As VP, Human Resources, U.S. Food Service, performed **strategic recruitment** and the design of a Management Development Program; produced six top leaders for challenging markets.

- Proven experience in devising, implementing, and leading **succession plans** for training, development and refreshing the pipeline of management candidates and technical personnel.

- Experience **training director** with vision; expert in consulting with managers on required training, mission changes, and work demands.

My experience in these areas in private industry would provide a unique viewpoint from which to support those working in Small Businessa and Self-Employed programs at the IRS.

I would like to have the opportunity to offer my extensive experience to the Small Business/ Self-Employed Business Unit. I look forward to a possible opportunity to meet in person for an interview. Thank you for your consideration of my application materials.

Sincerely,

Deborah Thomas

Enclosures: Federal Resume and KSA Narratives

Facts to Know About Deadlines

- Applications for federal job vacancies will be accepted only while the vacancy is "open." Exception: Veterans with 30% disability can apply for positions after a closing date, as long as there is no selection made on a position. The veteran would need to email or write the HR specialist for this consideration.

- Most online submission deadlines are 11:59 p.m. Eastern Standard Time on the due date, but double check this on your announcement!

- It is recommended that you submit your applications at least eight hours before any deadline. Don't wait until the last two hours to apply, give yourself some time, because problems can come up and you need time to research application challenges.

- Beware: If you put your username and password in the system incorrectly three times, you could get rejected from the system. For USAJOBS you can create another user name and password within minutes.

- USAJOBS announcements: Check the "How to Apply" page for directions on deadline and how to apply.

- For most paper applications, the deadline is 5 p.m. of the time zone of the address of the agency. Beware: If you submit by fax, the fax could be busy. Do not wait until the last hour.

- Postmark by 5 p.m.: This means your package must be postmarked by 5 p.m. in the time zone of the job.

- Received by 5 p.m.: This means they must receive it by 5 pm in the time zone of the job.

- Mailing: It is best to send by Return Receipt Requested, so you have notice that the package was received in the mailroom.

- "Open" periods can range from a few days to approximately four weeks. "One month open" means that they are looking at lots of applicants. "Extended deadline" means they have not received enough applicants.

- Re-announced announcement with new deadline: They announced the same position again with some change. You would have to apply again.

- Open Inventory: Announcements that are basically database collections of resumes for future searches. The U.S. Navy and CHART system are mostly Open Inventory; so are the Air Force announcements through USAJOBS. The HR specialists use this system for searching for applicants. These are "real" jobs, but the deadlines and timeline for a contact is unknown.

- Open Until Filled: This is also a database announcement collecting resumes until they have hired a number of applicants for many locations.

- First Cut-off, Second Cut-off, etc. dates. If you can make an early cut-off, go ahead, but they will usually still view resumes until the last cut-off. The HR specialist will view the resumes collected on the cut-off dates.

- If you apply online, do NOT send the same package by mail.

STEP NINE
Make Sure to Follow Through

How Long Does It Take to Get a Response to My Application?

Right now, the Office of Personnel Management is working with agencies to reduce the length of the hiring process to a total of 45 days, from the closing date of the announcement to the interview date. In many cases, you might hear back from the agency within a month after the closing date on the announcement. If the announcement is "open continuous," then it could take much longer before a position becomes available to be filled.

What Happened to My Application Package?

Here are the various things that can happen to the position openings:

- The position could be FILLED. If you are one of the finalists, you will be contacted for a telephone or personal interview. If you were not selected for either the interview or the job, then you may not be contacted at all regarding your application.
- The closing date could be EXTENDED if they did not receive enough applications.
- The recruitment could go through certain steps (review of applications, qualified persons "certified," and interviews), and then the position could be CANCELLED due to budget cuts or if the announcement was written incorrectly. The announcement might be posted again. You will have to re-apply, because previous applicant materials are discarded.

Be prepared for the fact that you may spend hours on your package, and the announcement could end up getting cancelled.

Follow-Up Techniques Summary

Paper Applications

If you submit a paper application package and have not heard anything in 30 to 45 days, you could contact the person listed on the announcement by letter, email, phone, or fax. Follow the sample scripts provided in this chapter. Be informative, pleasant, persevering, and genuinely interested in the status of your application.

Electronic Applications

USAJOBS and some agencies have automated systems where you can check the status of your application, though not all automated systems provide information about applications received.

Online Applications

Tracking electronic applications could be easier in some situations but could also present a different set of challenges. For example, when a computer rates and ranks your application, it is difficult to get human feedback on shortcomings with your resume when you are not found qualified for a position.

Furthermore, agencies differ in their application management. For example, in the military sectors, the U.S. Army has an excellent system for tracking the activity that has occurred with your online resume in the database. You can view your resume online and also see how many times, and when, your resume has been "pulled" for an announcement. The U.S. Navy and Air Force also each have their own individual tracking systems as well. Therefore, if you are applying to an agency with an independent tracking system, check its website to learn more about how it operates.

Tracking Your Application on USAJOBS

For the most part, we will focus our discussion on how you can track your electronic application on USAJOBS, because this will account for the majority of the electronic applications submitted.

You can check the status of your federal applications online anytime. If you have an account in USAJOBS "My Resume," you can go to the "my applications" page where you can track and follow up with your federal applications. You can also check in the Office of Personnel Management's Questionnaire site, www.applicationmanager.ogov

When a federal agency uses USAJOBS to manage its resumes and applications, the human resources specialist will periodically update your resume account online. That way you can follow the activity in your applications.

Here are the typical responses that you may find, and ideas about how to handle each response:

- ✪ **Application started:** You began the application, but you did not complete it.

- ✪ **Application complete:** You applied correctly, but no one has looked at the resume yet. You will have to wait longer to see any activity on your application.

- ✪ **Announcement cancelled:** The job announcement has been cancelled for various reasons. It could be reposted, so check back periodically and apply again if you see a new announcement for the same position. They will not keep your resume on file.

- ✪ **Application pending:** The HR specialist pulled the resumes, and they are reviewing them now. You will have to wait for further action and the next note by the HR specialist to see if you have been referred to a selecting official.

✪ **You are not minimally qualified or you do not meet minimum qualifications:**
The HR specialist reviewed your resume, questionnaire, and profile, and you are not even minimally qualified.

Here are possible reasons:

- You do not meet minimum qualification requirements listed in the vacancy announcement, such as work experience, education, or selective factors.

- You applied for a job that was only open to current federal employees or other applicants with special eligibility, such as veterans or former federal employees.

- Your original profile in USAJOBS has something checked off that takes you out of consideration. For instance, you may have checked off that you will not accept any term position. You will not be considered if the job is a non-permanent position.

Now what do you do?

- Find the vacancy announcement if you still have it.

- Review your resume against the announcement.

- Review the Work Experience section of your resume (especially the last eight years).

- See if the Work Experience section demonstrates that you have the specialized experience for the position. If not, continue to work on the resume and re-submit.

✪ If you **are qualified**, this is very good news. Your resume and questionnaire met the minimum qualifications. What do you do now? Wait to see what happens next. You could be in the running to get referred to the supervisor.

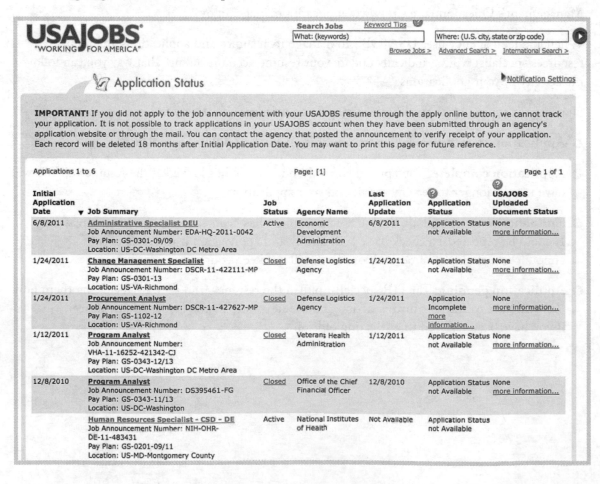

- ✪ **Your application was not referred:** Based on your responses to the questions, you did not receive a score high enough to be referred to the selecting official. The minimum score for minimum qualifications is 70. You may have scored more than 70, thus meeting the minimum qualifications, but did not rank high enough to be considered "best qualified" and referred to a selecting official. The highest score for most applicants is 100. Veterans can add a five- or ten-point preference and achieve the highest score of 110.

- ✪ If you are **referred to a supervisor or referred for selection consideration**, this means that your resume is on the supervisor's desk, and you are a finalist for an interview (if they interview for the job) or for an offer. What do you do now? Wait to see if you get called for an interview.

- ✪ You may also **receive a job offer online**. Congratulations! Though most job offers will come by phone or e-mail by the human resources specialist recruiting this position, the USAJOBS Application Manager or the Army's CPOL answer tracking page can actually offer you a job online, even without an interview. Occasionally supervisors do not interview people for federal positions, especially at the GS-9 level. Also, you may see the job offer here after the HR specialist calls and offers you the job. What do you do now? Do not accept the offer on the phone the minute they call you. Thank them and sound very pleased and upbeat. Ask if you can think about the offer for a day and call back the next day with your response. You need to review the position, salary, location, and benefits and determine whether you will negotiate your job offer.

- ✪ If you are **called in for an interview:** Read *Step 10: Interviewing 101*!

Application Manager

Main | Important Links | Help | Logout

user: ktroutman

My Application Packages
(Click VacancyID to see a checklist of all the items you need to complete your application package, and the status of each.)

Vacancy ID : 145961 Job Title : SPECIAL ASSISTANT

Status	Modified Date	Closing Date	USAJOBS Control Number
See Details Tab	7/19/2007 8:31:03 AM	07/19/2007	949266

Vacancy ID : 400211 Job Title : MAIL CLERK

Status	Modified Date	Closing Date	USAJOBS Control Number
Closed - Not Submitted	3/10/2011 5:05:27 AM	04/30/2011	2081166

Vacancy ID : 456557 Job Title : IT Specialist (Policy-Planning)

Status	Modified Date	Closing Date	USAJOBS Control Number
Closed - Not Submitted	4/11/2011 12:41:37 PM	04/11/2011	2224607

Vacancy ID : 457094 Job Title : Program Analyst

Status	Modified Date	Closing Date	USAJOBS Control Number
See Details Tab	5/24/2011 2:06:57 PM	05/26/2011	2223688

Vacancy ID : 460232 Job Title : Writer/Editor

Status	Modified Date	Closing Date	USAJOBS Control Number
Closed - Not Submitted	5/6/2011 3:00:38 PM	05/11/2011	2258182

Vacancy ID : 468133 Job Title : Workforce Recruitment Program Administrator

Status	Modified Date	Closing Date	USAJOBS Control Number
See Details Tab	5/14/2011 2:40:56 PM	05/14/2011	2258510

Vacancy ID : 468227 Job Title : Program Analyst

Status	Modified Date	Closing Date	USAJOBS Control Number
Closed - Not Submitted	5/6/2011 12:02:42 PM	05/06/2011	2248829

Paper Applications: You Mean I Can Contact HR?

Most federal job applicants are not aware that they can contact the HR personnel handling their application. Asking questions, gaining information, developing a relationship, and becoming known are helpful parts of the application process. You can track and follow-up on most of the steps your application follows in the system. Some of the online application systems are even set up to ensure that you will be contacted.

Vacancy announcements typically include the name of a human resources contact responsible for many aspects of the application process. This HR person may have created the vacancy announcement, may have posted it on USAJOBS and other websites, and may communicate with the hiring supervisor. They may coordinate the review of the packages and be part of the rating and ranking process to determine who will get an interview. This HR person is a great resource for you.

Just a reminder, they are busy!

Human resources staff are occupied with multiple announcements, various aspects of announcement development, reviewing packages, and responding to supervisor needs. Use diplomacy and consideration when contacting them about your package. Your goal is to be remembered favorably!

If you are told by the HR office that you were not rated "qualified" and you feel you really were, you can ask for reconsideration. Agencies have different procedures for this, but it's probably best to ask in writing to the attention of the Human Resources Officer. Your rating (or non-selection) is unfortunate, but mistakes do happen. The office will not be able to consider any new information, only what you submitted with your application.

How to Contact the HR Person

- **Telephone:** You probably will not reach the HR person with your first call, so be ready with a good voicemail message. Practice your message before calling.

- **What if you try calling and there is continually no answer?** If the phone is always busy, or you leave a voicemail and never receive a call back, here is what you can do: research another vacancy announcement with the same agency (preferably at the same grade level), look for a contact name and phone on that announcement, and call him or her. They are probably co-workers and this person may be able to tell you what happened to the recruiter you are seeking. It is possible that they changed jobs, are on vacation, or are on detail to another agency. HR staff people are usually very helpful and informative. And, they may be able to answer your question themselves.

- **Email:** By all means, use this method if it is recommended.

- **Fax:** Sometimes only a fax number is provided. In this case, write inquiries simply and clearly, making sure to include your contact information.

- **No personal contact information:** If there is no name or personal contact information, but there is an address, you may write a letter. If there is no address but a database, you cannot contact anyone. Just submit your application and cross your fingers.

Human Resources Specialist's Insight

"Customer service is not what it should be in many HR offices—we just don't have enough people. If you have not sent your application by some method that gets you a receipt, I would call the agency and make sure they have your application. I have seen applications get misfiled, put in wrong folders, and otherwise mishandled. If you are calling four weeks later and the agency did not get your application, it is too late to do anything about it. Also (and most readers of this book will not make this mistake), if you are calling before the final due date, you can make sure that the HR office has everything it needs (DD214, SF-50, performance appraisal, and so forth) to consider you. In our office, if you don't submit necessary paperwork (say DD214 for VEOA jobs), you're out—we're not going to call you and ask for it."

Sample Scripts

Follow Up

"Hi, Ms. Rogers, this is Kathryn Troutman from San Diego, CA. I'm inquiring about my application for Writer-Editor, GS-7, announcement 20205, which I submitted on April 5, 20xx. I'd like to know the status of my package, or when the packages are being reviewed. Can you please return my call, or leave a voicemail at (410) 777-7777? The best time to reach me is 8 to 10 am. Thank you."

You Have Been Told You Are Not Getting the Job (Telephone)

"Hello, Ms. Rogers, this is Kathryn Troutman. I got the notice that I was not hired for the job (Announcement 20205, Writer-Editor). When you have a few minutes, I would really appreciate your help with knowing why I was not selected. I'd really like to work for the government in your agency and I felt I was perfectly qualified. If you could take a few minutes and call me back or leave a voicemail, I would appreciate knowing what I could do improve in my resume or my qualifications for future applications. Thanks so much for your help. My number is (410) 777-7777. The best time to reach me is 8 to 10 am."

You Are Getting an Interview – Congratulations! (Telephone)

"Hello, Ms. Rogers, this is Kathryn Troutman. Thanks so much for the opportunity to interview for the Writer-Editor job, announcement 20205. I am very pleased! I would like to know if you can give me some insight into the interview system. Will there be one person or a panel interviewing me? Also, will the interview follow specific questions? And if so, would I be able to receive these questions ahead of time? I am beginning my research and preparation for the interview now. I look forward to this opportunity. Thanks for any information you can provide! My number is (410) 777-7777. The best time to reach me is 8 to 10 am."

After the Interview – Thank You Note!

Dear Ms. Rogers:

Thank you so much for your time last Wednesday. I enjoyed meeting you and hearing about your agency. I believe that I would be an asset to your organization and feel certain that I would be able to learn quickly about your mission and programs.

I look forward to your decision and hope that I can begin my career at the Office of _____ at the Department of _____.

Thank you again.

Sincerely,

Kathryn Troutman

Sample Questions for Applicants to Ask Human Resources

1. Can you clarify something from the announcement for me?

If you do not understand exactly a certain request in the vacancy announcement, ask for clarification. If the person you are talking to is not the named contact person, be sure to get his or her name.

2. Have you received all my materials?

Many vacancy announcements require you to submit materials by different methods. For example, you may have to use a Quickhire online application system which follows two steps: 1) submit information online, and 2) fax or mail your transcripts. It is a good idea to check to see if all your materials have been received before the closing date. Some electronic application systems, like CPOL, list the status of your application materials. If you mail any materials, remember to save your receipts.

3. What is the status of my application?

The federal job application process can take a while. You can call to check on the status of your application, but we suggest that you wait about a month after the closing date. You may learn that you did or did not get on the list submitted to the selecting official, or that interviews are being conducted.

4. How can I improve future applications?

This is REALLY IMPORTANT. If you learn that you did not get referred for a position, ask the contact person to tell you what you should do to improve future applications. You may learn that you missed a selective factor. You may learn that you were not qualified for a particular grade. You may learn that you did not score highly on your KSAs. You may also learn that you scored very well, but were in competition with a highly qualified group of applicants.

The HR representative usually will not go into great detail, but may tell you what your overall score was, where your KSAs were weak, and where you ranked among the pool of applicants. If you did not get the job you were seeking, then talking on the phone with the people who read and scored your materials can be the most valuable five or ten minutes you can spend in this whole process.

STEP TEN
Interviewing 101

Key Points

This chapter contains a large amount of information to digest. Here are the key points to remember:

The Behavior-Based Interview Is a Test

The interviewers will score you on each question and your answer. They will have a scoring sheet in front of them while you are talking. Be prepared for the "interview test" with your accomplishment answers and knowledge of the mission and position.

The Government Interview Is Normally 30 to 45 Minutes in Length

Typically the panel or individual interviewer will ask five to ten open-ended questions based on the knowledge, skills, and abilities required for the position. Be prepared to give examples that will demonstrate that you have the experience to perform the job. Answers should be one to three minutes in length. Time yourself when you practice.

Know the Paperwork

Know the vacancy announcement, agency mission, and office function. Read your resume and KSAs out loud with enthusiasm. Become convinced that you are very well qualified for the job and that the agency NEEDS you to help achieve their mission.

Do the Necessary Research

Go online to research the agency, department, and position. Read press releases about the organization. Go to www.washingtonpost.com and search for the organization to see if there are any recent news events.

Practice

In front of a mirror, tape recorder, video camera, family member, friend, or anyone who volunteers to listen to you.

Confidence, Knowledge, and Skills

In order to "sell" yourself for a new position, you have to believe in your abilities. Read books and listen to tapes that will help boost your confidence and give you the support you need to "brag" about your work skills.

Types of Interviews: 3 Basic Formats

Interviews may be conducted in person or over the phone, and may include an interview panel. Interview elements may include several categories, including:

- ✪ Behavioral
- ✪ Technical
- ✪ Competency

Behavioral Interviewing

Be prepared for a new interview format, the Behavior-Based Interview. Be prepared to give examples in your answers to seven to ten questions that will be situation- or experience-based. If you have an example of how you led a team, provided training, or managed a project, be prepared to talk about the project and teamwork. The best answers are examples that demonstrate your past performance.

You will see typical questions that could be asked in most interviews. Most panel members or individual supervisor/interviewers will prepare seven to ten questions. The same questions are asked of all the interviewees. The answers are graded. So, be prepared to give examples that demonstrate your knowledge, skills, and abilities.

If you have written your KSAs from Step 7, the KSA narrative/examples could be the basis of your accomplishments for the Behavior-Based Interview. However, you will have to practice speaking about your accomplishments. Even the most seasoned speakers, briefers, and media experts take training in speaking, presentation, and content development. Jobseekers should spend more time writing examples (their "message") that support their best strengths, and practice speaking these elements.

Behavioral Interview: Sample Questions

- "Your supervisor has left an assignment for you and has left on a weeklong vacation. The assignment is due when she returns. You do not completely understand the assignment – what would you do?"

- "You have been responsible for dealing with a particularly challenging client, who has indicated in their latest phone call that they are thinking of taking their business someplace else. How would you handle the situation?"

- "The successful candidate for this position will be working with some highly-trained individuals who have been with the organization for a long time. How will you approach them?"

Tips for Preparing for a Behavioral Interview

Prior to the interview, spend some time identifying behaviors that would be critical to success in the position—and do an honest assessment!

Do a "Google" search and look for behavioral interview questions—and practice!

Spend some time thinking through mistakes you have made in the workplace. What would you do differently—in other words, how would you change your behavior the next time?

Technical Interviewing

Technical interviews are focused on providing the selecting official with additional information regarding the technical or functional skills of the applicant.

Sample Questions

- "Describe your experience with accounting principles, practices, and techniques."
- "Describe your experience in applying program management theories and processes."
- "This position requires experience in scientific research—provide us with information on your role and/or participation in performing basic and/or applied research."
- "How do you keep abreast of new developments in your profession or industry? On a scale of 1-10, how up to date are you?"

Tips for Preparing for a Technical Interview

Closely review the technical requirements listed in the vacancy announcement, and develop a mental inventory of your skills for each requirement.

Check with college professors, peers, and counselors regarding information on the technical challenges and issues facing the organization; develop scenarios for problem-solving!

Competency Interviewing

A competency interview is an employment interview in which the competencies have been defined by the organization, and in which applicants are asked questions to determine their possession of the competencies required for the position. These interviews may seem like the behavioral interview described above.

Sample Questions

- Problem Solving: "Give me an example of a time when you had to develop a new solution to an old problem."

- Teamwork: "Describe a time when you used your teambuilding skills to gain buy-in for a project or idea."

- Communication: "Describe a time when you had to communicate under difficult circumstances, either verbally or in writing."

Tips for Preparing for a Competency Interview

Spend some time thinking about mistakes you have made on the job or in school—how would you explain them to an interviewer—and what have you learned from those mistakes.

Research the organization's website to identify organizational competencies and values, and assess how you would fit into the organization.

Research practice questions and work with peers or counselors to practice responding to questions.

Types of Interview Questions

In addition to the different types of interview questions already described, you will likely get additional questions from some of the categories listed below:

Traditional Questions

The standard interview questions ask what you would do in a given situation. These questions are more hypothetical and allow you to give best-case answers; they concentrate little on your actual experience.

- "Tell me about yourself." (An all-inclusive question. Also "Why should I hire you?" or "What about this job interests you?" Keep this response job-related and refer to your KSAs and competencies. Give a two-minute commercial selling yourself for the position.)
- "Describe a major obstacle you have overcome."
- "What are your strengths?"

Situational Questions

Similar to the behavior-based questions, these questions are not so much questions as they are scenarios or situations you could encounter in the new job. The interviewer is looking for how you would react and respond to these situations.

- "We are always looking for new ideas to increase productivity, improve morale, and reduce costs. Tell me about an idea you have that could yield positive results."
- "If you were to go in and find a center not running as efficiently as you expect it could, what would you do?"
- "You find you double scheduled your manager for two appointments at the same time. How do you handle the error an hour before the appointments?"

Difficult/Negative Questions

These questions put you on the spot. They can be designed to increase your level of stress to see how you will respond. The questions themselves should be answered by giving the most positive responses you can and by showing ways you are trying to improve.

- "What are your weaknesses?" (List only one. Let the interviewer ask for more.)
- "Tell me about a time when your work was criticized."
- "Describe a difficult problem you've had to deal with." (Best to keep your answer work-related, not personal)

Illegal Questions

Not mentioned as a possible format, these are questions that should not be asked and do not need to be answered. Interviewers should not ask any questions regarding race, gender, religion, marital status, sexual orientation, or national origin.

Unanswerable

If you are asked an unanswerable question, the best thing to do is to be honest. Refocus on something you can do and demonstrate how you can meet the position's specific needs.

Types of Interviews: 3 Basic Methods

Telephone Interview

The telephone interview can be either a pre-screening interview or the full interview, as though you are sitting in the office with the supervisor or the panel. During a telephone interview, you can have notes in front of you to help you with your responses. Just do not rely too heavily on the notes—you do not want to sound as though you are reading from a script. Remember, the Selecting Official is mainly interested in determining whether you should be invited to participate further in the process.

Tips:

- Get dressed comfortably
- Be prepared, relaxed, and confident
- Have your resume and the announcement in front of you
- Create your skills and accomplishments list and have it with you
- Be seated in a quiet room at a big table
- If you are on a cell phone, make sure it is clear and has plenty of battery power

Individual/One-on-One Interview

You may be invited in for a face-to-face interview with the Selecting Official and/or other members of the staff or Selection Panel. In a few cases, especially when a candidate or an interviewer is unable to attend the face-to-face interview, a more formal interview can be conducted by telephone. If there has been no pre-screening interview, the face-to-face interview will be the first step in your interview process. The face-to-face interview can be either individual/one-on-one or group/panel. You may be called in for a preliminary interview (either individual or group), then be invited back for another (or multiple) interview(s) with the Selecting Official, staff members, and/or members of the Selection Committee who will then meet and make a decision regarding your qualifications.

This type of interview is often conducted across a desk in a question and answer format. However, in recent years more interviewers have opted to make the experience more comfortable. They may have each of you sit in chairs on the same side of the desk and make the dialogue more conversational. This all will depend on who is conducting the interview.

Group/Panel Interview

The third type of interview is the group/panel interview, during which you are interviewed by two or more interviewers who are directly related to the position (supervisor, co-workers, subordinates), members of the department, and/or members of the Selection Committee. Usually each member of the panel has questions to ask, but there have been interviews where only one person has done the asking, and the others involved are there simply to observe.

Tip: If given a choice, try to get a seat at the end of the table so that you can make eye contact with more of the panel members.

Parts of the Interview

During the actual interview, you can anticipate spending between 30 minutes and one hour with the interviewer or panel. Some interviews are shorter; others can be as long as several hours to a full day. Often, you will be told in advance how long the interview should be. The interview typically begins with introductions and an explanation of the position. It then moves into a question-and-answer session where you are asked a majority of the questions, and ends with an opportunity for you to ask some questions about the position.

Opening

This is your opportunity to make a good first impression—first impressions do count, and the first two minutes of the interview are critical. They will make the interviewer decide if he/she wants to keep paying attention to what you have to say. A good deal of small talk typically occurs during this time as you and the interviewer(s) get to know each other. Again, you will be given some background about the position, and this is often when you will be asked the first question, something usually along the lines of "Tell me about yourself."

Body

As you move into the body of the interview, you will be asked a number of questions (traditional, behavior-based, competency-based, situational, difficult, etc.) that will help the interviewer(s) determine your KSAs, competencies, and experience in relation to what the agency is seeking for the position at hand. In general, when responding to questions, you always want to provide examples demonstrating your KSAs and competencies. Your specific experiences and examples will set you apart from the competition, and your ability to effectively articulate how you are the best candidate for the position can make all the difference in whether you receive an offer for the position. In other words, you want to be able to show them, not just tell them, why you are qualified. Confidence in describing increasingly more responsible and complex assignments and experiences translates into good marks on the interviewer's "scorecard," used to compare the candidates. If the interviewer has to pull information from the candidate, the resulting impression is weak.

Closing

At the end of the interview, you will be given an opportunity to ask questions or bring up any selling points that were not discussed during the interview. Take advantage of this opportunity. If at the end of the interview you feel you have not had the opportunity to elaborate on a particular experience, explain a relevant skill, or demonstrate a specific expertise, now is the time to do it. If you have a portfolio with examples your work, you may bring it to the interviewer's attention at this point if you have not already. Do not take up too much time; it is, after all, the end of the interview. Nevertheless, do not miss an opportunity to sell yourself for the position.

Once you have asked your questions, and made any extra points, do not forget to thank the interviewer for his/her time and reiterate once again your qualifications for the position. This will enable you to leave on a high note—summarizing your qualifications one last time so the interviewer(s) will remember at the end of the interview why you should be the candidate hired for the position. You may also ask when you should hear back from them and let them know you will be looking forward to that.

Questions to Ask the Interviewer

By all means, ask questions of the interviewer. The questions you want to ask the interviewer should be ones you are truly interested in getting answers to. You will want to limit the number of questions you ask at the end of the interview to no more than four. If you are interested in something the interviewer talks about during the interview, ask about it. Questions encourage dialogue, and dialogue can make the interview more conversational and more comfortable. Again, do not overdo it. The questions you ask should help you determine whether or not this is the right job for you.

In order to prepare questions in advance, take a look at the Position Description (PD) and KSAs—is there anything you would like the interviewer to explain or elaborate upon? See if you have generated any questions from the research you have done. Be careful that you do not ask questions that you should already know the answer to (something listed in the PD, for example).

Have ten questions prepared for the interviewer. Only ask the ones that were not addressed during your discussion.

Here are a few general examples:

- ✪ "What is the most significant challenge of this position?"
- ✪ "What is the most important contribution you would like to see made in this position in the next two months?"
- ✪ "Are there opportunities for creativity and problem-solving skills to be put to use?"
- ✪ "Beyond the job description, what are the expectations of this position?"

After the Interview

Thank you letters should be written graciously, promptly, and carefully. Think about the best form for your thank you. If the interviewer tells you they plan to make a decision that night, then you should email promptly. At the same time, if you are applying to an agency that prides itself on doing personalized work for clients, you may want to send a handwritten message on a nice card. Either way, thank the interviewer for their time, gently reminding them of your interest in the position and the valuable contributions you would bring to the organization. Do not miss that last chance to market yourself!

Nonverbal Communication

It is also important to think about your nonverbal communication when you are preparing for the interview. First impressions are made immediately based upon how you entered the room, whether or not you made eye contact, and how you presented yourself through your dress, habits, and mannerisms. Needless to say, nonverbals can significantly influence the interview.

Here are some non-verbal pointers to keep in mind:

⊛ Entrance. Exude confidence.

⊛ Handshake. Should be firm, but not too aggressive.

⊛ Personal grooming. Clean, neat, professional dress, and do not overdo makeup, cologne/perfume, or jewelry.

⊛ Tone of voice and volume. You want to sound interested (with inflection), no monotone; but do not be too boisterous, overbearing, or funny.

⊛ Eye contact. Maintain eye contact with the person you are speaking to. During a panel interview, look at the person who is asking the question. It is acceptable to look up while you are thinking, or to look around at each of the interviewers, but you want to avoid staring off into space, keeping someone in a deadlock stare, or constantly moving your eyes from person to person as if you were at a tennis match.

⊛ Enthusiasm. Act like this is the job for you. No one wants to hire someone who is not excited about the opportunity. Just do not come across as overzealous.

⊛ Posture/body language. Do not slump back in the chair. Do not get too comfortable because this can suggest boredom or lack of interest. However, do not seem too eager, whether by sitting on the edge of your chair or invading someone's personal space.

⊛ Nervous habits (fidgeting, repeating the phrases umm and ahhh while you speak, shaking your leg, playing with a pen or paper, taking your glasses on and off, etc.). We all have nervous habits. During an interview your goal should be to minimize yours. That is why practice is so important—it helps you identify what your nervous habits are. Identification is the first step to eliminating the habit. For example, if you find that you play with items in front of you, do not have them there during the interview.

⊛ Smile. Again, you want to be as positive as you can throughout the entire interview.

Steps to Prepare for an Interview

Step 1: Find and print the target announcement.

Step 2: Analyze the job description.

The interviewer will base questions on job analysis. Job analysis is the process of looking at a position (or, more broadly, the work of an organization) to identify essential functions and duties, and the competencies, knowledge, skills, and abilities needed to perform the work.

Step 3: Prepare your answers.

Prepare a one-minute response to the "Tell me about yourself" question. Write five success stories to answer behavioral interview questions ("Tell me about a time when…" or "Give me an example of a time…"). Prepare answers to the most common interview questions that will best present your skills, talents, and accomplishments:

- Why did you leave your last position?
- What do you know about our organization?
- What are your goals? Where do you see yourself in 5 years?
- What are your strengths and weaknesses?
- Why would you like to work for this organization?
- What is your most significant achievement?
- How would your last boss and colleagues describe you?
- Why should we hire you?
- What are your salary expectations?

Step 4: Research background on the agency and office—learn the latest news and challenges.

Here are a few ideas to jump start your research:

- Find the mission of the organization from the vacancy announcement
- Find the agency's website; look up the history of the agency and other news
- Research any recent events with the agency or office at http://www.govexec.com/ and www.washingtonpost.com
- What are the major issues or concerns of the agency?

Step 5: Read about interviewing for federal jobs.

Study this chapter, but you can also look online for even more information.

Step 6: Practice, practice, and practice your interview techniques.

Practice in front of the mirror or with a friend for feedback.

Step 7: Be confident in your research and your ability to do the job.

Final Tips

Before the Interview

⊛ Try to find out what kind of interview to expect, i.e., behavioral, technical, etc.

⊛ Remember nothing will make you look worse than not knowing what you put on your resume.

⊛ Get your references' permission to use them as references. You can ask former managers, professors, friends of your family (but not family members), or people who know you through community service. Provide your references with the following information: the job for which you are applying, the name of the organization, and a copy of your resume.

During the Interview

⊛ Arrive 10 to 15 minutes early for your interview.

⊛ Dress appropriately! Ironed clothes, including skirts (at knee length or longer), nice slacks, or a suit. Keep your interview outfit simple and professional. Be conservative.

⊛ Carry these items to the interview: A copy of your references (for which you already have permission); paper on which to take notes; directions to the interview site; a copy of your resume; and a pen.

⊛ Be aware of your body language and eye contact. Stand and greet your interviewer with a firm handshake and a smile. Crossed arms appear to be defensive, fidgeting may make everyone nervous, and a lack of eye contact may be interpreted as a sign of an untrustworthy person. Instead, nod while listening to show you are attentive and alert, and sit and stand upright.

⊛ Think before you answer; if you do not have a clear understanding of a question, ask for clarification. It is okay to take a moment to pause. If you need more time, ask to have the question repeated. But only do this once.

⊛ Express yourself clearly and with confidence, not conceit. Keep your answers concise and to the point.

⊛ Show a sincere interest in the office and position.

⊛ Highlight yourself in your examples and stories, not your co-workers or supervisors.

⊛ Focus on what you can contribute to the organization rather than what the employer can do for you. Do not ask about salary or benefits until the employer brings it up.

⊛ Do not start a political discussion.

⊛ Do not place blame or be negative about past employers.

⊛ If some volunteer work you have done demonstrates a specific skill, use that experience as an example. To demonstrate your qualifications, you may go beyond your professional experiences to draw on other relevant examples.

⊛ Be honest. Too much embellishing, or falsifying, is a serious mistake.

⊛ End the interview on a positive note indicating how you feel you are a good fit for the position at hand, and how you can make a contribution to the organization. Ask about the next step, as most offers are not extended on the spot.

⊛ Thank the interviewer and ask for a business card. This will provide you with the necessary contact information for following up.

Negotiating for a Federal Job

Final Words from the Author and Federal Career Coach, Kathryn Troutman

Congratulations on being offered a position with the federal government! Here are a few final tips to help you negotiate your job offer.

JOBSEEKER QUESTION:

I received a call from a human resources specialist with a job offer, but I did not accept the job on the spot. I asked if I could take some time to think about the salary and benefits, and then call back the next day. The salary range for this GS-9 position is $39,795 to $51,738. I currently make $44,000. How do you go about negotiating for the higher salary range? What factors go into the agency's decision?

KATHRYN'S ANSWER:

You can negotiate certain financial benefits with the supervisor who is recruiting this position. Keep in mind that you will need to prove superior skills to receive a higher step than Step 1.

Each government job has a range of salary and grade or pay band. There is a range that the HR specialist and supervisor may have in mind to offer you—depending on your years of experience, specialized experience, and critical skills, and the budget of the agency. You should have NO PROBLEM getting $44,000. I personally think that a person should strive for a minimum of 10% increase for a new position, so I would say that you could ask for $48,000 for this job.

Also, keep these following points in mind:

Government Pay Scale Information

Check out the General Schedule Pay Scale page at http://www.opm.gov/oca/08tables/html/gs.asp.

Ask for a Higher Step Within Grade If You Can Prove Superior Skills

You do have the ability to negotiate your Step within your grade level. You can request a GS-9 Step 7 ($47,757), or any step you choose, based on any of the following reasons:

✪ Wanting a 10% raise from your previous salary for career development and advancement objectives.

✪ Proving that your salary was $44K or higher with a W-2. This can help the supervisor see your objective in negotiating for a higher step.

✪ Statingthat you have extensive expenses involved in travel and relocation to the new position (because they might not specifically pay for the relocation expenses).

✪ Demonstrating that you have specialized experience that will greatly benefit the agency upon your hire into the position.

- Having critical, superior skills, education, and abilities that will greatly enhance the agency's mission and office services.

- Needing a minimum of Step 7 ($47,757) since you will be relocating to a geographic area with a higher economy, requiring additional income to support your family and needs.

- Providing any additional reason you can think of to justify why you should be paid more.

Request for Tuition Reimbursement for Student Loans

Some agencies contribute payment toward student loans: up to $500 per month or $10K per year (up to $60K total). You may be able to get the tuition reimbursement if the agency has the funds or accepts the program for new hires. You can read about the government policy for hiring incentives at http://www4.law.cornell.edu/uscode/5/5379.html.

Critical Hiring Need or Severe Shortage: Recruitment Bonus Incentive

Some agencies may pay a recruitment bonus incentive for Critical Skills or Severe Shortage positions. Each agency is different and some may have critical job shortages. The agency could pay up to 25% of the annual salary. You can read the definitions of Critical Hiring Need or Severe Shortage at www.opm.gov.

Request for Relocation Allowance

If the vacancy announcement does not state that they will NOT pay for relocation, you can ask if they will pay for relocation costs. If the announcement says that they WILL NOT pay for relocation, then you will not be able to negotiate this point.

Be Confident

Be confident that you are highly skilled, ready to commit, and dedicated to public service. When you ask for your higher step, tuition reimbursement, or other request, you should be confident that the government WANTS TO HIRE YOU. They have selected you and they do not want to start the hiring process over!

Negotiating Is Negotiating

When you negotiate, do not worry that they will take away your offer, because they will not. But remember that there is also no guarantee of any agreement to your requests. This is pure negotiation. If you have justifiable reasons and expertise for the job, you might be able to settle on agreeable terms. Keep in mind that you do not know about the budget the office has for hiring this position, so there could be unknown financial considerations for the agency.

Good luck with your negotiating! Please write to me if you have any recommendations or success stories for negotiating with federal human resources specialists or supervisors.

INDEX

About the Author

KATHRYN TROUTMAN

Kathryn Kraemer Troutman is the founder and president of The Resume Place, Inc., a service business located in Baltimore, MD, specializing in writing and designing professional federal and private-sector resumes, as well as coaching and education in the federal hiring process. For the past 30 years, Troutman has managed her professional writing and consulting practice, publishing and federal career training business, and with her team of 20 Certified Federal Resume Writers, The Resume Place advises and writes more than 300 federal resumes per month for military, private industry, and federal clients worldwide.

Internationally recognized as the "Federal Resume Guru" by federal jobseekers and federal human resources specialists, Troutman created the format and name for the new "federal resume" that became an accepted standard after the SF 171 form was eliminated in 1995. She is the pioneering designer of the federal resume based on her first book, the *Federal Resume Guidebook*, which already is in the fifth edition.

Troutman is an in-demand, government contract federal career trainer, who has trained thousands of federal employees in writing competitive federal fesumes, KSAs in the fesume, Senior Executive Service applications, and USAJOBS applications for more than 175 federal agencies in the United States and Europe. Her Federal Career Training courses and publications are listed on the GSA Schedule for government agency purchase. Her popular website, www.resume-place.com, receives more than 50,000 visitors per month, and provides online tools to assist with federal resume writing and federal job searches to jobseekers worldwide.

Troutman created the Certified Federal Job Search Trainer program—the first ever federal career train-the-trainer program for career counselors and military career counselors—using the popular curriculum, Ten Steps to a Federal Job, based on the award-winning book by the same name. Since 2002, more than 500 career counselors and workshop leaders have been licensed to teach the Ten Steps curriculum. In addition, the 62 U.S. Navy Fleet and Family Support Centers worldwide teach this curriculum to separating and retiring military personnel and family members as part of the Transition Assistance Program (TAP). U.S. Air Force, Coast Guard, and Army military transition centers use the Ten Steps Jobseeker Guide (workshop handout) and curriculum to help military personnel write federal resumes and submit to Resumix databases.

Some of Troutman's other federal career publications include the *Federal Resume Guidebook*, the award-winning *Student's Federal Career Guide*, and the *Military to Federal Career Guide*, which is used in every Navy and Marine Corps base and most Air Force career transition centers in the world.

Troutman is a Federal Career Coach to federal, military, and private sector jobseekers who are striving to achieve their first job in government or get promoted. She is a Certified Career Management Coach with specialized expertise in government careers and advises executives in achievement of Senior Executive Service ranks, as well as career management and growth for all career levels.

A frequent radio, TV, and online guest, Troutman answers questions about federal careers, resume writing, and job search techniques.

Get more expert help with your federal application!

FEDERAL RESUME WRITING SERVICES—Your federal resume is your most important federal career document. After you read this book and look at the samples, consider the professional services of expert federal career consultants and federal resume writers.

CERTIFIED FEDERAL RESUME WRITERS AND THE OUTLINE FORMAT—Our signature Outline Format designed by Kathryn Troutman is preferred by federal human resources specialists, because they can easily find the information they are seeking.

FEDERAL CAREER CONSULTING—Advice and recommendations on federal positions and occupational standards to match your experience, education, and specialized knowledge. Get the latest up-to-date strategies on how to market your past experience into new careers in government.

SENIOR EXECUTIVE SERVICES ECQs—Our expert SES writers and consultants can help not only make your decision about pursuing an SES position but also in develop the best possible ECQs for your application.

More Information:
www.resume-place.com
(888) 480-8265

From the Foreword to the Federal Resume Guidebook, 5th Edition:

"So – what's the savvy job applicant to do? Clearly, they will need to do their homework and pay close attention to the relevant details about the job and the application process contained in the announcement for each federal job in which they are interested. Simply submitting the same boiler-plate resume and cover letter to every job one sees is not going to be nearly as successful as a carefully tailored response that speaks to the specifics of each job.

… **Kathryn Troutman** has literally made a career out of understanding and tracking the evolution of the federal hiring system and translating that understanding into practical advice for the job seeker."

John Palguta
Vice President of Policy
Partnership for Public Service

Free federal career info! >> *Visit www.resume-place.com/resources*

- Free webinars about federal resume and federal career consulting services
- Free webinars on Hiring Reform and how it will affect your federal job search
- Free KSA, Federal Resume, and Cover Letter Builders
- Up-to-the minute federal job search info—register for our informative newsletter
- Federal job search news articles, updated daily

Brought to you by:

Kathryn Troutman
Author, *Federal Resume Guidebook*
President and Founder of The Resume Place, Inc.
The Leading Federal Career Consulting and
Federal Resume Writing Firm in America

Need More Help with the Ten Steps?

Try our easy-to-use online training course,
based on the second edition of this book.

With audio, videos, and interactive quizzes, Kathryn will walk you through and explain her book, *Ten Steps to a Federal Job*, 2nd Edition. Easily learn the Ten Steps to a Federal Job™ designed by Kathryn Troutman to help jobseekers navigate the federal job application system.

The Ten Steps curriculum is currently being taught by career counselors and federal agencies worldwide. Now, you can access this invaluable course material without ever leaving your desk. No software or additional programs are required – just you, your computer, and an Internet connection.

New version of the course for the Ten Steps to a Federal Job 3rd Edition
coming soon!

www.resume-place.com/books/ten-steps-online-course/

Award-Winning, Best-Selling Career Books by Kathryn Troutman

FEDERAL RESUME GUIDEBOOK 5th Edition—Newly revised in 2011! Perfect for federal to federal jobseekers. This book is nearly 450 pages of comprehensive, in-depth guidance on how to craft the perfect federal application to change jobs or get promoted. The *Federal Resume Guidebook* is THE book that created today's federal resume.

MILITARY TO FEDERAL CAREER GUIDE 2nd Edition—President Obama has created a new program to hire more vets into the federal government. But even if there are more jobs, applicants STILL have to write a competitive federal resume. This book is designed to help you translate military skills and competencies into the federal skills, keywords, and an outstanding resume.

THE NEW SES APPLICATION—New release for the summer of 2011! Aspiring to join the elite ranks of the Senior Executive Service (SES)? Master the key steps involved in the SES applications: writing the traditional ECQs, Technical Qualification narratives, 5-page SES federal resume, executive cover letter, and executive interviews.

JOBSEEKER'S GUIDE 4th Edition—The *Jobseeker's Guide* is the first-ever publication for military and family members who are seeking federal employment. This best-selling publication is the accepted training handout in TAP classes and employment courses at Military Transition Centers worldwide and is utilized in more than 100 military bases around the world. This publication is also the featured guide supporting the Certified Federal Job Search Trainer program for career counselors on the Ten Steps to a Federal Job.

CREATING YOUR HIGH SCHOOL RESUME 3rd Edition—Throughout this workbook, students will respond to straightforward questions about their skills and interests to help them build their resume section by section. Several case studies and samples show students firsthand how to focus, organize, write, format, and use their resumes. Students will learn how to format their resume using electronic tools, how to use the Web and email effectively for researching and finding contacts, and how to manage electronic resume files.

STUDENT'S FEDERAL CAREER GUIDE 2nd Edition—New release for the summer of 2011! This book is a must-buy for students, new graduates, young professionals, parents, college career centers, and career counselors. Details the winning 10-step process for going from the classroom to a federal job. Includes basics like our federal employment glossary, tips on salary negotiation, and a step-by-step guide to the behavior-based interview.

More information and secure online ordering:
www.resume-place.com
(888) 480-8265